D0459498

ORBiT

As a noun, an orbit is one celestial body under the influence of another. The moon is in orbit around the Earth. The Earth is in orbit around the Sun. This is all because of the influence of the larger body.

As a verb, to orbit is to "revolve around"—
To be *under the influence* of the other entity.

Tides, Seasons, Days, Sunrise, Sunset, Birthdays, Weather.

To ORBiT is to be influenced.

ORBiT

THE ART AND SCIENCE OF iNFLUENCE

ORBiT

THE ART AND SCIENCE OF
iNFLUENCE

DAN MANN

THE**MANN**GROUP

Printed and Bound in the United States of America.

ISBN: 978-0-69-284716-9

First edition First printing.

Edited by Barry Lyons
Cover and Interior Design: Stewart Williams
Author photo: Steven McBride
Library of Congress Control Number: 2017902308

DEDICATION

To my children, the light and loves of my life:
Meghan, Rebekah, Hank and Kent.

PRAISE for
ORBiT—The Art and Science of Influence

I have known Dan for almost 30 years. I met him as a young adult and at a time in when I had very few positives influences in my life. He was the most influential person I had ever met. I watched Dan influence an entire school and improve the lives of countless young men and women. Dan led many of my friends and me into a personal relationship with Jesus Christ. That influence changed us for an eternity. The ability to influence people can literally change the world. We all know people in our society that have an extraordinary ability to influence others, but very few have the ability to explain the "art" of influencing adults the way Dan has so eloquently done in this book. Whether you are trying to influence a corporate team of 500 or just an individual that you care deeply about, Dan's book lays out an excellent road map filled with practical application on how to become a successful influencer. While reading the book, I found myself constantly sharing excerpts with my team. By the time I was finished, I decided to make it required reading for all current and future leaders within in my organizations. Truly one of the best books I have ever read.

TODD OUELLETTE,
President and CEO of Long-Lewis Automotive Group

CONTENTS

FOREWORD

've always been a teacher. It may be my default behavior. Looking back, every time I learned a new skill, for some reason, I set about to teach it to someone.

My bachelor's degree is in theology. My first real job out of college was at a small church in Selma, Alabama. The church had a private school—Meadowview Christian School. In addition to my duties at the church, I also taught in the school. Even though I was just 21 years old (three years older than the seniors), and looked 16, everyone called me "Mr. Mann." I was originally slated to teach Bible as a history course. The headmaster needed an art class, so—of course—I volunteered to teach it. The school had never offered a music program, so I started a choir. And as you'll see in Chapter One, I helped coach a few of the sports teams. Since I had played guitar from the age of 12, numerous students approached me to teach them guitar. The choir needed a drummer, so I taught Wade Akers, one of my students how to play drums, even though I had never played drums myself. The local YMCA wanted to offer karate classes, so naturally, I took up that project, having studied karate throughout my college years.

Those four years of my career were formative for me. I was teaching, but it's really the case that those students at Meadowview taught me how to teach. Every minute of every day I was teaching someone something. It became a way of life and set me on an approach I would use over and over throughout my career. In many ways I owe this skill of influence to those special students from the late seventies at Meadowview Christian School.

In 1991 I went to work for a men's fashion retailer in Memphis, Tennessee (Bachrach Men's Clothing). I pursued the job because it paid eight percent commission. I needed money. Having never sold before, I had to pick it up quickly. My district manager, Paul Lequire, took time with me to role play some selling scenarios. I was comfortable with this learning style, so I picked it up and did relatively well. After six months of selling, Paul offered me the opportunity to manage one of the stores in his district: Hickory Ridge (046).

I knew nothing about managing a retail store. I knew nothing about managing sales people. Heck, I knew nothing about fashion. What I did know was how to teach. So, I set about doing the one thing I knew how to do. I taught.

- I taught selling skills
- I taught product knowledge
- I taught company policy
- I taught customer service

Of course there were ups and downs, but after six months, the store had experienced its highest increase in five years: a 25 percent growth. On the strength of that growth, I received another promotion to district manager, supervising 10 stores. Once again, I knew nothing about multi-store supervision. I knew nothing about marketplace development. But, I did know how to teach, so I set about teaching the managers of those stores how to teach:

- How to teach selling skills
- How to teach product knowledge
- How to teach company policy
- How to teach customer service

Over the next five years, these stores collectively increased 15 percent—best in the company. This performance led to my eventual promotion to Vice President of Retail, and the supervision of all 75 stores. Training your people pays off. This investment—when done right—produces returns multiple times over. But influencing people only happens when you, the influencer, are prepared, disciplined, and intentional.

It can be very difficult for people to change, learn, or grow. Habits, doubts, and lack of discipline often prevent people from making the changes they seek. So, I've come to the conclusion that people need help to achieve their own goals. Adding this skill to your leadership approach helps you to achieve *your* goals—and helps others achieve theirs.

INTRODUCTION

THE SIX STEPS TO INFLUENCE

Leadership. Leading. Lead. Lots of people talk about it. But there are too few people *doing* it. That is probably because we may not know what it "looks like" when it's happening. Assemble a random group of business people in a room and ask the question: "What are the attributes of leadership?" Whenever we ask, the answers we receive are often a group of mushy, ambiguous concepts like "inspiring," "attitude," and "confidence."

I certainly agree that these are great descriptors of leadership, but my experience tells me that all too often we don't know exactly what these attributes look like. We know them when we see them, but if we aspire to become leaders, we eventually need to learn how to turn these ideas into action. Inspiration becomes measurable when it translates into action and those actions translate into results.

> A leader is best when people barely know he exists, when his work is done, his aim fulfilled, they will say: We did it ourselves. —Lao Tzu

Students regularly fail to recognize great instruction when it's happening. Many of us have a tendency to look back at a period of time in our life and realized that there had been someone of great leadership who was central to our development. For example, a great teacher often guides us to self-discovery. A great teacher helps us learn. A great teacher provides opportunity for development. While it's happening the student may not even be aware of it. Social media is filled with people who are attempting to track down that elementary school teacher, band director, coach, or camp counselor who was especially important—it "only" took a decade or so of perspective before they could come to realize it!

So you could say that this experience is more about the student choosing to learn and less about the teacher teaching. Still, it is the leader who understands the *need* for learning. The leader understands what's at stake. The leader sees the lack of performance in the student—and the potential.

Often, the leader's biggest challenge is developing a student's desire to learn. Without the desire, the teaching may be great, but actual learning is absent.

Take Responsibility

Blame. It sure feels good, doesn't it? There's no need to accept responsibility. It's *their* fault! When someone in leadership blames the members of their own team for failure, the whole team suffers. You may have heard these kinds of excuses used by managers:

- "They don't get it"
- "What's wrong with these people?"
- "He's lazy"
- "People just don't care anymore"

If you're in leadership or management, you have no option to use these excuses. You must accept responsibility for your team! You must create the outcome you want! You have to initiate change. *You* are in your role for a reason: You are charged with leading and influencing others to achieve the needed results. If your team "doesn't get it," I would ask, "How come? Why haven't you helped them understand?" If you say your team "doesn't care anymore," I would ask, "Have you offered a compelling reason for them to care?" If you say you're team is "lazy," you're going to get another question from me: "Do they understand what is expected of them, and what's at stake?" My good friend, Todd Ouellette (owner of Long-Lewis Ford in North Alabama) says, "There are no bad people, just bad processes." His upbeat point of view is a function of his confidence that getting results is dependent on him influencing his team.

Why do some restaurants always seem to get it right, meal after meal? Even though there is turnover with the wait staff, hosts and kitchen staff, still, time after time, the experience is consistent and memorable. Don't all restaurants understand the sanitation codes? The flavor principles of good tasting food? Don't all restaurants know that patrons expect their order to be delivered accurately and in a timely manner? Of course they do. The restaurants that stand the test of time have leaders who have successfully hired and influenced a team to do the right things every time.

In January 2010, I was in New Orleans conducting a strategic planning session with Dave Zimmer and the leadership from Fleet Feet Sports. For dinner one night we went as a group to NOLA, Emeril Lagasse's restaurant in the French Quarter. It was a fantastic meal. One of the most memorable experiences of the night was the following.

Even though there were 10 of us dining, each time a new course was presented, all plates were carefully set before each guest at precisely the same moment. Now you know that at most restaurants one server brings out a tray with everyone's meal. As a patron you're expected to sit while all plates are put out one at a time. Eventually, everyone gets their correct plate. But not at NOLA. Everyone at the table received their plate at the same exact time! Yes, this required five servers, each carrying two plates—but it was done with style, grace, ingenuity, and class. This did not happen by accident. I can only imagine the process and system it must take to organize this experience.
- Someone had to come up with this idea
- Someone had to devise the process that could make it happen
- Someone had to decide to implement it
- Someone had to enroll the staff to do this each time

- Someone had to teach the process

That person is the Leader with Influence, and that Leader created a literal "bam" experience for all of us at the table that evening.

Howard Shultz is one such leader. In January 2008, he took over Starbucks. At that time, Starbucks was a company that had over-expanded and, many felt, had lost its way. He intended to turn things around. He took responsibility for influencing change: changing behaviors, changing results, and changing the culture. What exactly did he do?

On February 26, 2008, the largest specialty coffee retailer in the US closed its doors three hours early. Starbucks closed all its US stores and dedicated the next three hours to emergency training! This decision cost the company millions in lost revenue and payroll. Why did they do it? So that their 135,000 US employees could refocus and practice in order to improve their *service*. Sure, their coffee is expensive. But most of their customers are there for the atmosphere created by their service. Starbucks wanted that focus returned to the forefront. Rather than place blame or offer excuses, Howard Schultz chose to influence his organization and its people in order to get a new result.

You can too. Blame and Excuse will not serve you well. Instead, choose Influence as your course of action.

- Lead your team
- Influence those around you
- Take responsibility for your own outcomes
- Get results
- Be effective
- Create change

And enjoy the success that comes with this type of life.

That success is simple. The people that you have influenced are *doing what you want*! They are acting in the best interest of your organization. You will have created a culture within your team—a culture that succeeds, a culture that executes, a culture that serves your vision.

Several years ago I offered a three-day sales training seminar to Big Peach Running Company in Atlanta, Georgia. The owner of BPRC, Mike Cosentino, is a real stickler for culture, execution, and customer service. Believe me when I tell you, it shows! Mike warned me in advance that his company refers to their customers as "guests." To help reinforce this concept, all BPRC employees carry the title of "Guest Advocate." Since this isn't my normal way of talking about customers and employees I slipped up several times and said, "employee" or "customer." Each time I was immediately corrected, *not* by Mike—but by numerous members of his leadership team! His managers owned the culture. In order to make this happen, I'm sure Mike had to set the standard. He likely repeated his expectation dozens of times. Over the weeks and months that preceded my training, Mike had been successful at influencing his team. The result? A culture change—and new behaviors.

CHAPTER ONE

Behavior Change Is A Process— And The First Step Belongs To You

MEADOWVIEW VS. MORGAN

My first job after college was teaching at a small private school in Selma, Alabama. It was small enough that if you were male and a teacher in the high school, that qualified you as a member of the coaching staff of the football team. (Once again, this is Alabama.) This particular year, this team was not good. We had gone through the first nine games of the season with a 1-8 record. But the final game of the year was against the crosstown rival, Morgan Academy.

The week leading up to the big game was filled with a variety of pep rallies, parades, banners, contests, and every other possible technique to "rally the troops." Going into Friday, the team was fired up. As (bad) luck would have it, someone from the rival school decided on Thursday night that they would spray paint a variety of taunts and insults—in Morgan Academy's school colors—on the walls of our school.

Well, now the football players were whipped into a frenzy seldom seen in central Alabama. In the locker room just prior to taking the field, the head coach, Mike Shipp, offered the single most inspiring pre-game speech in history. His speech would have made

Disney proud. He referenced every possible motivation to win the game: family, country, school pride, World War II, legacy and, of course, manhood.

We screamed, we yelled, we whooped and we ran to the field. Bolstered by our confidence, our boys took the opening kickoff and returned it 98 yards for a quick score: 6–0.

We lost the game, 53–6.

In fact, we never crossed the 50-yard line again that night. The Meadowview Trojans were not a very good team. Yes, they went on to win state championships in future years, and Mike Shipp enjoyed a hall of fame career coaching high school football. But that night, we didn't have the talent, skill, or strategy to beat a much better team.

I learned a valuable lesson: Inspiration alone isn't enough. Real results are possible only when inspiration is combined with the correct action.

TAKE ACTION!

There are few emotions that can match the awful feeling of powerlessness and the realization that nothing will change, that no matter what you do, things will remain the same. As you read this, think back to the times you've felt that way, especially if you've been in a leadership position where you are responsible for results. Whether you're a sports coach, an entrepreneur, a division manager, a teacher, or a CEO, you're likely charged with getting those results through others. In this role, you must know how to influence. You must be confident that you get your team to embrace your ideas and your strategies and make progress together. Initiating action and creating change falls on your shoulders.

So, why do teams fail? Why are managers ineffective? Why do things remain the same? Consider this:

- People fail because they have no context. They have no real understanding of the situation they are in and therefore have no motivation or sense of *urgency* to change.
- People fail because they take the incorrect approach. They've developed bad habits, see no reason to change, and are content to continue on that path because it feels easier than doing something different.
- People fail because they've never been introduced to the correct approach. They've never seen it done correctly, and therefore have no paradigm of the right technique.
- People fail because they haven't practiced enough. They've never invested the time and energy to develop the necessary skills to succeed.
- People fail because they've never had good coaching. Without proper guidance, feedback, direction, instruction, and accountability, most people can't find their own way to success.
- People fail because they never develop competence.
- Effective leaders initiate action. Instead of allowing hopelessness and powerlessness to creep into your belief system, take action. Exert your influence to change your condition. Achieve the results you want with a team. Become the leader everyone wants to follow. Relish the confidence you'll have to know that you can organize and influence change with your team. This can make you one of the most valuable, dependable, desirable resources in your organization.

But the first decision, the first step belongs to you. You must decide to *take action.*

WHAT IS ORBiT?

In October 2011, Boeing delivered its long-anticipated 787 Dreamliner, which ushered in a "new age of air travel." The key feature of this luxury cruiser is that 50 percent of it is made of "composite materials," including plastics and carbon fiber. It flies faster, farther, and is significantly quieter than any aircraft in history. But its sexiness is not limited to the technologies that make it fly. Each seat has custom entertainment on a 17-inch touchscreen! The windows are 30 percent larger and are controlled by a button instead of a shade. There's more room for bags—and they've even improved the air handling system to remove offensive odors more effectively at 35,000 ft. This aircraft is certainly the latest evolution in air travel technology.

But this multi-billion dollar modern marvel won't take off without an important piece of equipment that costs $1.25. What is it? A *clipboard*. The pilots are in place surrounded by the best technology in the air. But the pilots will not take off in this miracle of modern engineering without first going through their pre-flight checklist (which is attached to the clipboard). In this technical, electronic world even the greatest advances rely on a process.

In the realm of influence and behavior change, you'll find that a simple process can help you be more effective too. In 40 years of teaching I have found a process that works. This approach helps you make progress, monitor your trainee's adoption, and build accountability for results in both the teacher and the student.

I call it ORBiT, which is an acronym (pronounced like "orbit") that means **O**ptimized **R**eality **B**ehavior **T**raining. Let me break it down:

Optimized: to carry out with maximum efficiency

Reality: real or contrived situations without a script

Behavior: the range of actions by people in relation to their environment

Training: improving one's capability, capacity, productivity, and performance.

ORBiT is a six-step process designed to:
• Secure Buy-In
• Set Expectations
• Increase the urgency needed for change
• Create agreement on the approach
• Resolve any misunderstanding on how to do something

• Teach technique
• Develop skills
• Increase proficiency

Throughout this book I will use four words—which are often used as nouns—as verbs: teach, lead, coach, and influence. Sometimes I will interchange them, occasionally even in the same sentence. I do this because influence requires some elements of all of these actions. Notice the interrelations: Teaching often requires coaching, coaching implies influence, influence means that you lead, and leading shows that others are looking to you for guidance.

ORBiT is the Six-Step Process to Influence

Today, the ability to influence is one of the most marketable skills a manager can possess, and the ability to influence is vital for anyone who wants to accomplish their vision through others. It is especially required for anyone who has a worthwhile cause.

You may never have thought of yourself as a leader, teacher or coach, but if you're reading this book, you must understand the value of being an effective influencer. Each of these six steps, taken separately, is important in life. It's when you put them all together—in this order—that you can be assured of a buy in and competence. You will have influence!

You will see the overview of this process in a diagram on page 19

Why don't other training methods work as well? And why is this method better?

Video

Using videos for training and development has been around as long as there have been videos. This enables a "one to many" approach to training. A teacher can communicate to students all over the world without ever leaving the studio (or living room). The student can access this information at their convenience and watch the training multiple times, increasing retention. With an investment in production, the trainer can create a powerful, emotional presentation that's enjoyable, entertaining, and effective. So what's the problem?

First of all, using video limits the amount of time you can spend training. As entertaining as they are, most people will not spend more than 12–15 minutes watching a training video. The attention span for learning today is shrinking. Look at the top ten most popular videos on any given day on YouTube. They usually vary in length from 45 seconds to seven or eight minutes. Most of them average around four minutes.

Second, video is usually a one-way communication. The trainer has no assurance that the student has bought in to the message, no assurance that the student will adopt any new behavior. Several years ago we revamped the training program for a sporting goods retailer that had previously attempted to use video training. The company had created a full library of several dozen training videos. There were numerous problems with the videos: production quality was bad, and most of them were more than 30 minutes in length. Worst of all, no one in the company was following up or monitoring the videos. They were surprised to find that even though there were more than 350 employees in the company, none of the videos had more than seven views!

Too many organizations that rely on video training sleep peacefully at night believing that their work force is well trained because they have "state of the art" training. They shouldn't.

Shadowing

Shadowing—a work experience option where students learn about a job by walking through the workday as a shadow to a competent work—is especially popular as a training option for restaurant and retail workers. Managers like it because it's free (at least they think it is). It's quick, and it requires no materials or infrastructure. I believe too many managers like it because they don't have to do anything. I don't like it. Let me break it down and explain why:

When an adult is being trained through shadowing I see *three* people being put in an awkward situation:

1. The person being trained: This person is relegated to being a shadow. How does it feel to follow someone around and to watch without an opportunity to interact? To many people this understandably might feel like punishment.

2. The person doing the training: You have someone following you around watching your every move. The pressure is on! I doubt that you'd be able to act naturally or offer your normal contribution to the job.

3. The customer being served: If this were a customer service environment, there would also be a customer present. How does the customer feel who is paying for service and is now included in a training exercise? I've personally experienced this scenario numerous times in restaurants. Picture this: Your server walks up to your table and says, "Hi, I'm Jenny. I'll be your server today. This is Randy. He's new and I'm training him today." She whispers some instruction to him and then turns her attention back to you. "May I take your order?" This is awkward (to say the least).

No confirmation of agreement is another training methodology that assumes a buy-in. Just because your trainee watched you do something (from the shadows) doesn't necessarily mean that they agree with the approach or that they will adopt the new behavior. In fact, as they are watching the "trainer" perform a task they may be saying to themselves, "I would never do it that way" or "Wow, I can't do that!"

Finally, there's this reality: The trainer is not a trainer. This is my biggest objection to shadowing. Most of the time when I see shadowing chosen as the training method, it is done out of convenience or desperation—a last ditch effort. So the manager chooses the best *performer* of the task, not necessarily the best *trainer*. So you have created a potential situation where neither of the people in the shadowing "training exercise" want to participate.

Some years ago I was checking into a hotel in Nashville where there was some shadowing training occurring at the front desk. This was a busy Friday night: high energy, lots of people checking in, and tons of time pressure. (What a great time to train!) The young lady who was being trained welcomed me and immediately apologized: "I'm Alice and I'm in training, sorry." In fact, her nametag communicated all of that. It actually read "Alice: In Training."

Alice did a perfectly good job of checking me in despite being visibly nervous. But when I asked her to input my loyalty number she got stuck; she hadn't been shown how to do that. She reluctantly leaned over to her shadow-instructor and said, "Ms. Johnson, can you help me with this?" Ms. Johnson was not happy. She literally moved Alice out of the way by forcefully taking her place in front of the computer screen and put her hands on the keyboard. She looked up at me and said, "I'm so sorry, Alice is new." She then loudly instructed Alice on the proper procedure as if I wasn't there. Ms. Johnson was not a teacher and did not want to be one. I doubt Alice stayed in that position very long.

Leading by Example

Initially, "leading by example" seems like the ideal method for behavior change. You think to yourself, "I'll just go out there and do a great job. I'll keep my head down and focus on doing the work. The team will see what I'm doing and will naturally want to imitate my approach. If I do the right things, my team will follow my example."

Let me be clear: Leading by example is vital to your success as a leader. You must be doing the right things in order to build trust, have credibility, and be seen as authentic. If you aren't leading by example, it's likely that you aren't leading at all! However, leading by example does not go far enough. Here are the potential dangers of *only* leading by example:

- The leader is doing all the work. You see this situation over and over again. The leader is so focused on doing the right things that she becomes the number one performer on the team, thereby making the highest level of contribution and failing to develop anyone else.

• The staff/students may be able to "see" the correct behaviors as the leader performs, but that doesn't mean they're able to replicate these behaviors. The leader who employs the "leading by example" method as their only approach to behavior change is often frustrated by the lack of results: "These folks just don't get it. Why do they continue to do this the wrong way? "Why am I doing all the work around here?" This type of leadership approach mistakenly believes it is getting progress in staff development just because they set the right example.

THE DIFFICULTY IN CHANGING ADULT BEHAVIOR

Human nature is complex, of course. Since I'm not a professionally trained psychologist, I don't intend to expound on the many layers of human psychology, motivations, behaviors, or to go into a discussion about nurture vs. nature. Instead, my goal is to offer a simple, straightforward methodology that has been shown to effectively help leaders influence their team. This approach does not manipulate. This approach does not succeed through force, policy, or fear of retribution. This approach recognizes that adults change their perspective—and behaviors—slowly. This approach addresses the reality that adults need to be involved in the learning process. We need to have *our* experience and opinions considered and included. Adults want context. Adults prefer to "try it out" before buying in. So the proper application of influence is respectful, collaborative, inspiring, challenging, and lasting.

Make no mistake: Asking—or expecting—adults to change their long-developed behaviors and habits can be a monumental task. These dearly held habits may have become foundational to who someone believes they can't do without them. Old ways will not disappear without effort and commitment. Adults have a very difficult time with change. It's not so much that we don't like change; it's actually more likely that we *fear* change.

So, if we're asking others to change, it is incumbent on us—the leader—to be the first one to do so. *You* will lead the effort in change. I would say that initiating the ORBiT process will be the first—and most difficult—change you have to make. If you've never worked this way before, if you've never put yourself in the role of leader, if you've never asked your team to reconsider their approach, if you've never attempted to be in a position of influence before, you will be making the first, and most important, *change.*

4. Demonstration
The Moment of Truth:
- Show Me!
- No Alignment=Poor Demonstration
- Poor Skills=Poor Demonstration
- Skill+Alignment=Performance
- Coach Observes and Evaluates

5. Feedback
- Self Evaluation

The Coach coaches:
- State the Positives
- Identify the Opportunities to improve
- Demonstrate again
- Clarify any misunderstandings

6. Cycle
- Drill
- Review/Evaluate
- Feedback
- Develop competence

1. Establish Context
Situation:
- What are we working on?
- Why?
- How long will it take?
- What's in this for me?

2. Negative Simulation
- Simulate Negative Behavior—let the trainee experience it
- *Emotion!*
- Ask for Agreement ("this is a problem right?")
- Trainee=Expert

3. Positive Simulation
- Simulate Positive Experience—Let the trainee experience it
- *Ah Hah!*
- Pop Quiz
- Most of all: *Alignment!*

5. Feedback

4. Demonstration

6. Cycle

3. Postive Simulation

2. Negative Simulation

1. Establish Context

CHAPTER TWO

Behavior Change needs a BIG reason why

ESTABLISH CONTEXT

If "Influence" interests you, then it is likely that you have a *cause*. Perhaps your cause is the betterment of mankind or a specific group with great need. Maybe that cause is as simple increasing your bank account or growing your company's market share. In any case, the question is *why* do you want to influence? What is the great cause that you need to enroll others to? I use "enroll" on purpose here. Enroll is a great verb. It's usually used in the context of going to school (enrolling in a course of study or at a university). So, enrollment:

- Is entirely optional
- Comes at some cost
- Represents a choice
- Indicates joining forces with others

When it comes to leadership and influence, enrollment acknowledges that the person you're working with must *want* to be influenced.

There's a wonderful scene in an otherwise forgettable movie, *Indecent Proposal*, starring Woody Harrelson and Demi Moore. Woody Harrelson's character is teaching a college class on architecture. He is projecting pictures of beautiful buildings and examples of compelling architectural design. Harrelson says, "If architects can just do their job and get it right, they can actually lift the human spirit, take it to a higher place." He quotes Louis Kahn saying, "Even a brick wants to be something. It aspires. Even a common ordinary brick wants to be more than it is." While he makes these statements he is scrolling through numerous pictures of inspiring architecture. skyscrapers, monuments, columns, spires, etc.

The scene depicts a truth: In the same way that a brick meta-phorically "wants" to be part of a grand design, each of us wants to be a part of something great. We want to belong to a greater cause. We want our contribution to make a difference. As you talk to your team about change it's important that you begin by addressing first things first: What is the big reason *why*? What is the larger vision? How does this change advance the cause? In fact, what *is* the cause?

In my early years at Bachrach Men's Clothing we struggled with this issue a bit. After all, it can be tough to attempt to motivate people by just saying, "Sell more clothes!" After giving it some thought as well as listening to our customers, we learned something. When a man prepares for a business meeting, a speech, a sales presentation, or even a date, he wants to be *confident*. Well, nothing destroys confidence more than looking unprepared. Mustard on a tie or having your pants unzipped can totally destroy your psychological preparedness. We learned that by dressing our customers well, we were actually delivering confidence. Once we understood that, and incorporated that language into our vision, our training, and our customer service standards, getting our staff on board was simple, easy to explain, and highly motivating.

So what's *your* cause?

If you've never spoken about a vision or a cause, this might be difficult. It may seem daunting to discuss the big picture. It may seem grandiose to be the guardian of a big dream. But, if you break it down into a series of questions that you have to answer, you'll be surprised at how simple and natural this conversation can be. Talking about your cause/vision isn't reserved for CEOs, politicians, or motivational speakers. You can—and must—include it in your process.

When discussing your cause answer these questions:

A. Why am I here?

Why have you decided that this is important to you? Why are you talking about this? How did you, personally, get to this point?

B. What about the past?

You may fear that your student is thinking to himself: "Right, but you didn't talk this way in the past." Well, you may need to address this. You may have an apology to offer. You may need to own up to past behaviors. If so, address this head on and don't be afraid to say you've made a mistake.

C. What is a vision?

The person you're speaking to may not have any connection to why a vision is important. Explain what it means to have a cause. Give some examples of great visions from the past: JFK and his vision of a man on the moon; Martin Luther King's vision of racial equality, "I have a dream."

D. What's your vision?

Now state in clear, simple—but earnest—words what your vision is. Only *you* can do this. Before you can influence someone or ask them to change behavior, they will need a clear and compelling reason why.

E. What if you don't get involved?

Few motivations are more powerful than the fear of "missing out." In Shakespeare's play *Henry V*, you can see this concept in his St. Crispin's Day speech:

And gentlemen in England now a-bed
Shall think themselves accurs'd they were not here,
And hold their manhoods cheap whiles any speaks
That fought with us upon Saint Crispin's day.

Paint the picture of the future—the future in which your vision is realized. Does this student *really* want to miss out?

F. What's your decision?

And so, you ask, do you want to work toward this future? Do you want to work on yourself? Do you agree that this cause is worth the effort?

No one is more prepared, more passionate or more authentic than you to share your cause. So before you begin any training, be certain you are convinced that the content is vital to your cause. Imagine the communication process as a game.

Here's the first great mistake that ineffective teachers make: failure to take responsibility for both sides of communication. That is, great leaders understand that they are just as responsible for the message being received as they are for the message being delivered well. You can imagine the communication process as a game of catch. Someone is "throwing" (or delivering information) and someone is "catching" (or receiving information). Just because you are a great pitcher doesn't mean that you will successfully complete the game of catch (someone throws and someone catches). If the person on the receiving end of the throw doesn't know how to play, or has never attempted to catch before, there probably won't be a successful catch.

Now, let's take this metaphor a little further. You and your "catcher" are on a game show. The world is watching. If the two of you somehow are successful at throwing *and* catching the ball just *one time*, you will both receive one million dollars.

If you want to be successful, you now have to take responsibility not only for your throwing, but also for the skills, interest, motivation, attitude, and performance of the person catching. *Your* success depends on it.

- Does he *want* to win a million dollars?
- Does he know *how* to catch a ball?
- Does he prefer that I throw the ball fast or slow, overhand or underhand?
- Does he understand what the word "catch" means?

- How far apart will we be standing?

It doesn't take much to apply this lesson to your role as a leader. An effective leader takes responsibility for both sides in communication. So, as you begin to communicate the context of your training to your student, you should check in.

- Does your student *want* to learn today?
- Does your student enjoy this type of learning experience?
- What else is happening in the life of this student?
- Is this the first time you've worked together like this?
- What is the existing relationship between the two of you?

You may have prepared and practiced your workshop for days. But if your student is not ready, engaged, and in the proper frame of mind for this experience, you may deliver like a professional, but there will be no receiving. The other side of the communication cycle hasn't been addressed or prepared. You'll be wasting your time—and hers.

ESTABLISH CONTEXT

Just to be clear, let's provide a definition of the word *context*: "The set of circumstances or facts that surround a particular event or situation, etc."

Many years ago, I was involved in a summer youth program at Camp Cyokamo in Carthage, Missouri. My role was to be one of the adult "camp counselors." We served many roles: team leader, teacher, coach, supervisor, lifeguard, and mentor. The dean of the camp was a great man by the name of Dick Thayer. One day, after lunch, several of us camp counselors were on the outdoor basketball courts playing basketball with some of the high school students. Leading the charge was another camp counselor, Craig Luper, a short, fiery, athletic ball of energy who was busy thrilling everyone on the court with his basketball skills, his humor, and his ability to generally entertain anyone who was within earshot. From his perspective, his role was to connect with the students, create camaraderie, and be seen as a adult who understands teenagers. He sincerely wanted to create the context of being approachable, likable, and fun.

I could see the confrontation coming when Dick Thayer walked out of the mess hall and crossed the yard to the basketball courts. He was red-faced and impatient. You see, from Dick's perspective, he had assigned every counselor to a specific clean up task after each meal. Craig wasn't doing his cleanup task: washing dishes. Instead, he was the playmaker in a pick-up basketball game, which was currently the hot ticket at Camp Cyokamo. Dick believed that the most important job for the camp counselors was to set the example of *service*. He wanted to show the campers that servant leadership is the path to success. He wanted all the campers to see his staff of adults washing dishes, sweeping sidewalks, cooking meals, and cleaning up the kitchen after each meal.

Their public argument did not serve either of them very well. While both of them may have had perfect logic for their activity and expectations, neither of them had properly established context nor had they achieved agreement from the other party in advance. If you intend to be successful at developing skills in another person, this person *must* first understand the circumstances.

"What's the situation we are in?"

"What are the facts?"

"What's going on here?"

Being prepared with those facts can help you make a great start. With Dick and Craig, the disagreement could have been avoided if both had agreed on the circumstances:

- Is it important to set an example of servant-leadership by performing maintenance around the camp?
- Is it important to play and have fun with the campers in order to develop relationships and connect?
- Should one of these be the priority?
- What is our approach to do both, if necessary?

Getting agreement on the context is the issue: You must have the facts, you must state the circumstance, and you must be prepared for your student to have an opinion on the issue.

If you intend to teach someone something you must address this basic truth: Adults learn differently than children. Fifth-grade students show up for class with the reality that they must learn the material and pass the course or run the risk of failing and coming back to the fifth grade again next year. Peer pressure, family pressure, and shaming all work to keep the student learning.

Adults don't have the same motivations. In fact, they may not even want to learn. In fact, in my experience, if your adult trainee doesn't see the need for the material they may take extreme measures to avoid learning it.

Some adults will make up reasons why they can't participate (I have to make a call!).

Some adults will sit on the back row and appear to be paying attention, but in reality are occupying their time with something else.

Some adults will attempt to manipulate the teacher with distraction or fogging.

Some adults will simply daydream and not physically participate.

So, what should you do if you intend to be effective? *You* must initiate the conversation. *You* must take responsibility for establishing the context. Take no chances. Assume nothing. Instead, be thorough. Be clear. Anticipate.

As the teacher, you should expect that your adult students are asking themselves these questions as you begin:

- "What are we working on?"
- "Why are we working on it?"
- "How long will this take?"
- "What's in this for me?"

Even though the student may not ask these questions out loud, failing to answer each of these questions will directly affect your results.

Let's look at them one at a time.

A. "WHAT ARE WE WORKING ON?"

Answering this question is as simple as a brief introduction to your session:

"Bill, we're going to work on some sales techniques today."

"Kathy, we're going to learn how to handle customer objections today."

This may seem completely obvious. But without context the student may not understand what you're doing.

"When you explain to people what you're trying to do, as opposed to just making demands or delegating tasks, you can build instant trust, even if it's just for that short time." – Simon Sinek

The first step to influence is to clearly communicate *what* you are going to be doing. Telling someone what you are about to do is an incredible communication tool. Even though you're not making a speech, there are some similarities in this circumstance to great speech writing.

- You must capture your audience's attention (even if your audience is only one person).
- You want to create interest in the subject.
- You want to engage your audience in the subject so they'll listen.

I initially learned speechmaking in college. My course book was *Public Speaking as Listeners Like It!* by Richard Borden. His recommended outline for writing and delivering a speech was simple:

- Ho hum
- Why bring that up?
- For instance?
- So what?

Any presenter expecting to be effective anticipates his audience's response in advance. Since we're talking about the beginning of your presentation, let's look at the first two in greater detail.

Ho Hum

If the presenter imagines his audience "starting at zero"—that is, with zero interest—he pictures the listener sighing deeply and thinking, "Ho hum! Do I really have to listen to this?"

The speaker's response is to open the speech with power, interest and even surprise. Thereby overcoming disinterest—and creating connection! No more Ho hum.

Johnny Pressley is one of the best speakers I have ever heard. Dr. Pressley is the chair of the theology department at Cincinnati Bible Seminary. I remember Johnny when he was a classmate of mine back at Roanoke Bible College (now Mid-Atlantic Christian University). Back in those days every student was required—sometime during the school year—to present a 15-minute speech during the all-important daily chapel service. These services were highly scripted, planned to the minute, and as somber as you would expect a southern Christian college chapel service to be. Hymns were sung (with organ accompaniment), prayers were offered. We stood and sat on cue.

Johnny walked to the stage and opened his Bible.

"I'd like to start today by reading a verse that has brought real meaning to my life, Ecclesiastes 10:1." Clearly, we're off to our traditional, somber start. "Dead flies cause even a bottle of perfume to stink, so a little foolishness spoils great wisdom and honor."

I can say with all certainty that this was the first time that dead flies had been brought up during a sermon in RBC's chapel. At first there was stunned silence from the audience. Then, an outburst of laughter. What is he talking about? Is that really in the Bible? Where is he going with this thought? Most of us students cut our eyes to our more conservative professors to see what their reaction was.

Johnny pressed on: "I don't know about you, but it doesn't take a lot of dead flies to ruin perfume. Just one will do. In fact, I'm the same way with a glass of water. It only takes one dead fly to spoil it for me."

At this point everyone was laughing. And guess what? He was on his way to making a great point: Even one small lapse in judgment will overshadow a lifetime of honorable living. But for that initial moment, no one in the room was saying "Ho hum." He had our attention and we were anxious to hear what was next. When you answer the question, "What are we working on today?" Be sure you do so with enthusiasm, energy, and excitement.

Why Bring That Up?

"Ok, you've got my interest. I'm intrigued and engaged. Where are you going with this thought? And what does this mean to me?" If my opening comment was effective at attracting attention, their next thought will be "I'm curious. Tell me more."

When you begin a training exercise, start with intentionality, and connection to your audience.

FORECASTING

Forecasting has numerous meanings. In business, it refers to making predictions of sales or manufacturing based on trends, data, and analysis. In meteorology, it's the science of predicting the weather.

For our purposes, forecasting is simply telling someone what you are about to do. As you begin your training, tell the trainees *what* you're going to be working on.

- Forecasting lets everyone know that you have a plan.
- Forecasting creates comfort: Others know what's going on.
- Forecasting sets the tone for the training exercise.

Consider how forecasting helps you everyday in your life. Imagine you're flying in a commercial airliner at 35,000 feet. Fight attendants are serving the passengers, while you enjoy a good book. Suddenly, the plane hits a patch of rough air: turbulence! Coffee spills, flight attendants desperately scramble to hold on and everyone is surprised and shaken. The pilot speaks over the intercom, "Whoops! Wow, so sorry about that folks. I hope everyone is ok. Sure didn't see that coming."

How are you feeling about the competency of the crew? How relaxed will you be for the rest of the flight?

Now, picture this scenario a little differently. You're flying in a commercial airliner at 35,000 feet. Fight attendants are serving the passengers, while you enjoy a good book. The pilot speaks over the intercom, "Folks, this is your captain speaking. We have some reports of turbulence about 10 minutes ahead. We're going to go ahead and turn on the fasten seat belt signs and ask you to return to your seats immediately and buckle up. I'll ask our flight attendants to do the same. We expect this turbulence to last only about seven minutes. We'll let you know when it's safe to move about the cabin again."

Sure enough, 10 minutes later, you hit turbulence, which lasts for seven minutes.

How are you feeling? While no one likes turbulence, you're probably feeling pretty confident about your captain's ability to get you safely to the gate.

It's all about forecasting. This creates awareness, includes everyone in what's happening and reduces stress due to a lack of control.

Nurses

Remember the last time you went to your doctor for a checkup? Your special time in that white-walled closet can be some of the most uncomfortable time of your entire year. A good nurse helps manage your discomfort by telling you—firmly and with confidence—what is about to happen.

"I'm going to step out of the room for 10 minutes. During that time please take off all of your clothes and put on this gown, tying it in the back. You can put your clothes into this plastic bag. I'll knock on the door before I walk back in. When I return the first thing we're going to do is collect a urine sample for a urinalysis."

I don't really want to do any of the things she said, but because she was straightforward and confident, I know this isn't the first time she's done this. Somehow this makes a difficult situation more comfortable.

Imagine if your nurse *wasn't* confident and asked for permission instead of forecasting.

"Um, Mr. Mann, would you like to take off all your clothes and wear this gown that's open in the back?"

"I know this is uncomfortable and awkward, but would you like to urinate into this cup?"

No. Comfort is created when we forecast exactly what is going to happen.

Not only does this create comfort, but forecasting also helps you establish confidence in the people you're working with.

Waiters

Good waiters know this already. Imagine how you would you feel if your waiter approached your table like this:

"Good evening, my name is Chad, I'll be your server. Would you folks like water for the table?"

"Yes, please."

"Also, we have some great appetizers. Would you like to hear about the specials on the appetizer menu also?"

"Sure, thanks."

"Would you like me to get the water first or do you want me to tell you about the appetizers first?"

"What?"

"Also, I could possibly go ahead and get your drink order. What would you like me to do first?"

Crickets.

You want your waiter to have a plan and forecast that plan to you throughout the meal. If they can stick to that plan—and do exactly what they say they are going to do throughout the experience—your meal is stress-free and satisfying.

If you intend to teach something, begin by succinctly stating *what* you will be working on.

What happens if you *don't* forecast?

The answer is pretty obvious: There'll be confusion and discomfort—which results in a distracted student and ineffective training.

Years ago there was a day where I found myself booked for two speaking engagements on the same day: During the day I was in Wichita, Kansas, and I was scheduled to be in Oklahoma City in the evening.

This was a defining moment in my career, in that I had allowed my client to book my travel. All I was told was that they would "take care of my flight arrangements." I wrapped up my afternoon session around 4:00. I knew that I was supposed to start the evening session in Oklahoma City at 7:00. Tick, tock, tick, tock.

I ask my client, "Who is taking me to the airport?"

"He's here, waiting for you in the lobby."

That's where I found him waiting for me (so far, so good).

"Are you my ride?" I ask.

"Yep, where are your bags?"

I load up into his car and we make small talk as we head toward the airport. As we pass the airport exit I had to ask,

"Which airport am I flying from?"

He replies, "Forgot to mention, I have to stop by my house."

Okay... so we leave town and head out to the Kansas countryside. As we arrive at his house, he says, "Come on in!"

Now, I'm nervous. "What time is my flight? I have to be in Oklahoma at 7!"

He shouts over his shoulder, "I just need to get my wife. She's going with us."

"Us?"

Moments later, he and his wife hurriedly emerge from the back room of the house—with their suitcases. (Now I'm really feeling the time pressure.)

"Let's go!," he says. "Help yourself to the Dramamine on the counter." Since I've never experienced motion sickness on a commercial flight I felt no need to take anything for it.

We walked out to the car, and I got into the back seat. My host and his wife kept walking, past the car and out to the barn. He slid open the large door and I finally saw it: a Cessna 172 Skyhawk.

"Wait, we're flying to Oklahoma City in *this*?"

He barely responded over his shoulder, "Yep. Put your suitcase in here."

But now I'm really confused. We're not at an airport; we're on a farm. There's no runway, no control tower, no gate agents. Just a plane and a barn.

I climbed aboard.

He started the engine and as his wife knitted in the back seat, he slowly began taxiing down the driveway. When the driveway ended he "merged" into a vacant field. "No way," I'm thinking. But, yes: He accelerates and slowly takes off from this field, barely climbing over a grove of trees at the last possible second.

This experience was hair raising enough as it was, but what made it truly stressful was that throughout the process I had *no* idea what was going on.

Forecast what you are going to do. This creates comfort, keeps the student engaged and reduces anxiety, making teaching--and learning possible.

One of my favorite scenes in a movie occurs about an hour into the 1984 classic, *The Karate Kid*, starring Ralph Macchio (Daniel) and Pat Morita (Mr. Miyagi). In the first hour Mr. Miyagi promises to teach karate to Daniel. He shows up on the first day expecting to practice kicking, punching, and blocking. Instead, Mr. Miyagi begins his first day by having Daniel wash and wax his cars. But he is very specific: "Wax on," he says, with his right hand in a circular motion, and then "Wax off" with his left hand in the opposite circular motion. Daniel is confused and challenges his teacher, but ultimately spends his first day washing and waxing four cars.

Daniel optimistically shows up for his second day of training. On this day, Mr. Miyagi instructs him to "Sand the floor." Once again the instruction is specific. "Right circle" and "left circle." This continues—to Daniel's increasing frustration—for days: "Paint the fence." "Paint the house." "Up, down"; "side to side".

Finally, Daniel decides to confront his instructor, "I'm tired of being your slave! I'm going home."

In one of the great moments of cinematic history (at least to me), Miyagi puts it all together: "Sand the floor, Daniel-san!" Miyagi punches as Daniel mimics the act of sanding the floor. Sanding the floor *blocks the punch*! "Paint the fence, Daniel-san" Painting the fence *blocks the kick*!

As Miyagi cycles through all of Daniel's previous chores, each one has brilliantly prepared him to stop all of the possible attacks by an opponent. Daniel didn't understand what he was learning. He didn't fully understand why he was being asked to do all these projects. But Miyagi did. And he knew where he was heading from the very beginning. So should you.

The second question we need to anticipate is:

B. "WHY ARE WE WORKING ON IT?"

This is the big question and it defines the situation you are in: Why are we working on this? Why is this important?

Let's start by defining the word:

Why: That which provides a reason, a purpose or justification. Synonyms:

- How come
- For what reason
- For what purpose
- What for
- To what end

You must anticipate the likelihood that one of the following questions will be a response from one or all of your students:

- "Why are we doing this?"
- "What is this anyway?"
- "Am I in trouble?"

Even if they don't make these statements out loud, you would be wise to anticipate that they are definitely thinking them. The strongest position to take in response is to consider why this situation matters to the organization. If you really want to understand the power of "why," you should connect it to your company's vision. This engages not only the trainee's head but their heart as well. It can also serve as an effective way to introduce the trainee's performance data because low performance results—and your commitment to improve them—can also provide you with a powerful "why." Simply put, training content without context is a waste of your time and effort. Bottom line: It's not effective.

In his book, *The 21 Irrefutable Laws of Leadership*, John Maxwell says, "The leader finds the dream and then the people. The people find the leader and then the dream." What makes a great leader? A great dream. A vision. A vision worth working for—and worth sacrificing for. Great leadership is always tied to a great vision. Effective influence is always tied to a cause worth achieving. If you expect to effectively influence others, you'll need to be certain as to *why*.

This actually calls for you—the teacher—to be clear about your purpose. How does this activity that you are about to lead tie to your overall vision? Even if your student is uncertain about "where this is going," it is crucial that you understand the "why."

When you have this clarity, you create a sense of urgency. But, picture the mindset of the adult you're about to train. They may be entirely unable to give you their attention. In fact, their point of view may surprise you. Here are some attitudes that are all too common:

• I have a college degree, I'm finished learning.
• I already know everything I need to know about this subject.
• Can I get by without this additional work?
• I'm an expert already. What can this person possibly teach me?
• I don't want to get better.

All of these attitudes can conflict with your efforts.

Even thought I'm not a pilot, I understand the concept of "landing in a crosswind." I fly 150,000 miles a year. Anyone who travels this frequently is going to experience an unpleasant landing when the weather isn't cooperating. You may have seen the videos of pilots landing in windy conditions. If not, let me briefly explain. Due to the configuration of the wings and rudder, the airplane is designed to fly straight. But when there is a crosswind, the pilot has to adjust course. If she doesn't, the airplane will lose control and crash. Perhaps you've seen videos of these types of landings. The airplane appears to be landing at the incorrect angle. The wings and fuselage are not aligned with the runway—the plane can appear to be as much as 45 degrees off center. The pilot has had to make significant adjustments to the plane's trajectory in order to safely land the plane. Landing in a crosswind is dangerous and requires skill and focus from the pilot.

If your trainee is uncertain about why your training exercise is happening, if your trainee doesn't see the value in the exercise, if your trainee doesn't understand how this exercise is connected to your cause—your training is like landing in a crosswind: dangerous and likely to fail. Their lack of alignment to your vision is like a crosswind. Their lack of urgency is like a crosswind. Their lack of focus is like a crosswind. Their attitude and point of view is like a crosswind. And it will likely make your training a waste of time.

You are most likely to succeed when you, your trainee and your vision are aligned.

C. "HOW LONG WILL THIS TAKE?"

It's a simple question, but one you should not overlook. As the teacher, you're asking an adult to give up their time, their freedom, and their control. That's asking a lot.

As you start the training be sure to clearly outline the time parameters:
- When are the breaks?
- When is lunch?
- When will we finish?

This will serve two purposes: First of all, this will actually relax your students. They can let go and trust you to manage the process. This allows them to focus and not be distracted with the schedule.

Secondly, this enables you to further establish credibility as a trainer. If you say, "This workshop will last 10 minutes"—and that is, in fact, what happens, your students can rely on your word in the future. Believe me when I say that nothing adds value to your training like starting and stopping on time.

In 1988 a young Democratic governor named Bill Clinton was tasked with making the nomination speech for Michael Dukakis. This type of speech is always a 10–15 minute affair, and that is certainly what all of the convention delegates expected when Clinton stepped into the national spotlight that night. In what has become known as "the moment Bill Clinton died on stage": Clinton delivered a 33-minute speech. The audience was through listening at the 10-minute mark. The remaining 23 minutes were spent uncomfortably as the entire convention—and the network news coverage—found something else to do. The most famous words in the speech, "In closing," were met with loud, sustained, and sarcastic applause.

Let your trainees know how long you will teach and stick to that timeframe.

The world of communication has become very sophisticated. If you're watching a video, you'll often see bullet points and the like. This keeps the viewer on track and adds reinforcement to the material—making it easier to remember. For most video these days, the scroll bar instantly tells the viewer:

- How long the video is
- How much time you have spent watching
- How much time is left

That's convenient—and it keeps the viewer engaged and in control.

When reading a book or training manual, the student also has control right at their fingertips. It's called a page number—another example of how the student retains some control over the process:

They know how far they've progressed and how far they have to go before finishing.

In the world of verbal communication, these tools do not exist and so there can be anxiety created when a student doesn't know the timing of the experience. You will greatly enhance your effectiveness if you forecast the parameters (in terms of time) in advance and faithfully stick to it. If you do this multiple times, your trainees will come to trust you. This trust enables them to listen better, remain distraction-free, and fully engage in your process.

My Dad was a preacher for 64 years. He started his ministry back in the days when services always started at 11:00 am on Sunday. It was expected that the service would be over by noon. In fact, North Carolina State "blue laws," which still exist, prevent the selling of alcohol on Sunday until after 12:00. I'm sure this law is a holdover from Prohibition. So to keep his audience engaged, year over year, he did two things really well:

1. He gave the audience his outline in advance. This follows the reliable speechmaking outline of

- Tell 'em what you're going to tell 'em
- Tell 'em
- Tell 'em what you told 'em

And,

2. He always ended at noon. No matter what else was happening, he finished at 12:00.

I remember a story he used to tell about a church leader who once gave him this advice: "Preacher, you can preach as long as you want to, but I'm going to stop listening at noon."

I guess he always remembered that. So should you.

D. "WHAT'S IN THIS FOR ME?"

Probably the most important component of this discussion is addressing this unspoken question: "What's in this for me?"

If you're leading, training, coaching, or developing people, they must be engaged in the process. They must care about what you're offering. They must want to learn! If wording it this way makes all of your students seem selfish, then simply reframe it this way: "How is this training connected to me?"

In my experience, the trainer has to be careful here not to make assumptions. In business, it's easy to assume that all students want to make more money. You could be making a mistake when creating a connection for your students by saying, "You will like this training session because it will help you make more money."

The fact is money is only one of many motivators that drive people. Look at these other categories of motivation:

- Individualistic (the desire for advancement and power). These folks are motivated to lead. They want to be in charge. They are looking for an opportunity for individual advancement and recognition. Think of politicians.
- Social (satisfaction from being on a team, working with people). These people love working with others. Naturally extroverts, they draw their energy and resource from helping others succeed.
- Aesthetic (motivated by beauty, design, art, and nature). The motivation for these people is found in structure and artistic expression. They might be interior or visual designers, artists, or even outdoors enthusiasts.
- Theoretical (driven by a desire to learn). This common motivation is found in people whose curiosity can't be quenched. They read, they study, they question, and they constantly learn.
- Traditional (actions are driven by a system of belief, such as a religion). These people adhere to a system of life in which an adherence to rules and guidelines is considered the highest value.

As you can see, these motivations are difficult to know without listening and learning from your student. In order to know "what's in it" for your student, you have to listen. Pay attention. Give the student an opportunity to speak.

Unless you know the motivations of your students it may be hard to connect your training to them.

Up to this point in the ORBiT process, you have been answering unspoken questions:

- What are we working on?
- Why are we working on it?
- How long will this take?

Which is to say that you have been doing most of the talking. You will now want to hear from your trainee. You'll need to ask, "What do you think is in this for you?" or "What do you think about this?" or "How do you think this could benefit you?" The goal in having your students answer any of these this questions is to get them excited about the learning—and to get them leaning forward, figuratively speaking, in their chair.

In general, when training, I find that trainers spend too much time doing the talking. Remember, adults *need* to be involved in the process in order for it to be effective—and for them to buy in. This is a hard lesson to learn, even for the best of us. When training, it is vital to get your student talking. You just never know what you might learn.

Several years ago I was conducting a manager training session for the leadership team at Big Dog Running in Columbus, Georgia. John Teeples and Reggie Luther are the owners of this unique retail business. I was working with the two of them and four of their managers. As usual, I started the day with introductions. When I arrived at one of the managers, she simply introduced herself by saying, "Hi, I'm Amy. I've worked at Big Dog Running for two years." Hoping to learn more, I asked, "Tell me about your running experience." She said, "Well, I ran in college at Providence." I replied, "Oh? What events?" She said, simply, "Mostly distance."

I never pass up a chance to brag about my kids. My youngest, Kent, was running track at UNC–Charlotte at that time, so I began:

"My son runs at Charlotte! Yep, he's a mid-distance guy. Loves the 800. In fact, he just shaved 1.5 seconds off his PR." I continued, "He went to the Penn Relays last year." Blah, blah, blah. I lost track of everything I said, but the entire time, Amy sat smiling, nodding and encouraging me to go on. Surely she was truly fascinated by my son's modest career.

At the end of the day, as we were walking out, John put his arm around me and said, "Dan, do you know who Amy is?" Well, of course I do. She's one of your managers—and a damn nice lady.

John gently revealed, "Dan, she's Amy Rudolph. Two-time Olympian. Former US Record holder in the 5k. Two-time US indoor 3000m Champion. Two-time US Cross Country champion. 1994 NCAA 1500m champion...." I lost track at that point as John continued. I had made the classic mistake of not asking the right question. I was so focused on my own story that I lost out on an opportunity to learn so much from the person sitting right in front of me.

I'll give Amy credit: she was so cool and calm. She sat right there and listened to my story about Kent as if it was the most interesting story she had ever heard. She smiled. She nodded. She seemed genuinely interested and impressed (which was the reaction I was hoping for—this is my son, after all). But at any time, Amy could have said, "Really? He runs the 800 at UNCC? Well, I've been to the Olympics. Twice!" Mic drop.

I learned a great lesson from Amy that day. When you're teaching, be sure you're asking the right questions. Be sure you are listening to your students. And sometimes, you'll have to work to pull out the real story from the person right in front of you.

CHAPTER THREE

Good Training involves some pain

NEGATIVE SIMULATION

This is the most difficult section for the trainer: creating a meaningful simulation.

On January 15, 2009, Captain Chesley (Sully) Sullenberger was the pilot on US Airways flight 1549 on its way to Charlotte, North Carolina, from LaGuardia in New York City. During its initial climb, the aircraft was disabled after striking a flock of geese. Soaring over Manhattan without power would cause most of us to be frozen by fear. But not Captain Sully. His quick thinking and precise actions saved all 155 passengers and every member of his crew. He ditched his plane safely in the Hudson River.

Chesley Sullenberger is a humble man. When he was interviewed about his heroism after the crash he said this:

"One way of looking at this might be that for 42 years, I've been making small, regular deposits in this bank of experience, education and training. And on January 15, the balance was sufficient so that I could make a very large withdrawal."

In other words, he had been training for that disaster his entire life. When it happened he was ready for it. Wow. That must be some training program. It is. You could make the case that the training for commercial airline pilots is the most sophisticated training methodology in existence today. How are pilots trained? Commercial airlines rely heavily on an advanced flight simulator, which allows the pilot to practice flying without actually flying.

"In a flight simulator, such as the Boeing 747 simulator, the control panel in a cockpit is identical to one in a real plane. Outside the windows, there are displays generated by the sophisticated computers, other wise known as computer generated images (CGI). When the trainee "takes off" in the simulator, he sees an identifiable airport and its surroundings. The simulation of Boeing Field, for instance, might show a fuel truck on the runway and Mount Rainier in the distance. The pilot also hears the rush of air around the wings that are not actually there. Besides, the simulator is tilted and shaken by six hydraulic systems. These are so convincing which make the trainee feels that he or she is actually controlling a real plane!" – Vincent Wong (Flight Simulation)

There are some significant advantages to the airline industry in using the flight simulator in training, as discussed by Nick Christiansen at aviationknowledge.wikidot.com):
- Novice pilots can experience simulated flight without risk to him or her or to valuable aircraft
- Simulation does not require a full flight progression, but permits repeated practice of a particular stage of flight (such as landing, for example)
- Risk-free introduction of flight challenges (systems problems, poor weather, wind sheer, etc.)
- Risk-free introduction of emergencies and systems failures
- Ability to replay and review a simulated flight or parts of it, matching performance against criteria
- Permits trainee to make and learn from mistakes without risk

So, in fact, Captain Sully was able to successfully land his plane in the Hudson because he had done it virtually hundreds of times before!

In fact, consider *any* training methodology where the training cannot fail. When the training *must* work, some form of simulation is involved:

1. Medical school students who are learning surgery practice their skills on cadavers. Once they are using the scalpel on a live patient, they have practiced surgery in a simulated environment hundreds of times before—except for the fact that risk was eliminated because the "patient," a cadaver, was not going to die.

2. The military continually creates simulations that mimic the real thing. Army weapons qualification courses, firing ranges, war games, submarine, tank, and aircraft simulators are some of the many ways that the military ensures its training works. In fact, after equipment maintenance and payroll, training is the largest line item in the US military budget. Where possible, most of it is simulation-based.

3. Teaching CPR in schools requires the use of an inflatable "manikin" which allows hundreds of students to experience a realistic simulation of life-saving technique—the best way to learn it!

4. How do pilots of 200-ton ships learn how to navigate into and out of ports or lock systems like the Panama Canal? At the Port Revel ship-handling training center in Grenoble, France, their trainees practice navigation using meticulously engineered 1:25 scale models of real cruisers, tankers, and containerships. These miniature boats, act, respond, and feel just like the real thing. This enables the pilots to practice their skills to proficiency without any risk to the larger, more expensive "real thing." Since 1967, Port Revel has trained more than 6,000 pilots in perfectly safe conditions.

5. The gigantic (and expensive) equipment needed for major earthmoving projects are difficult to master. For years, this industry has used simulators that are similar to the ones used by the airline industry. These simulators offer a controlled environment for

the new operator to safely experience the exact feel and response to the controls inside the cab. The simulator offers a realistic replica of the cab of an actual earthmover. This training method allows the trainee to develop proficiency without risk to people, equipment, or project.

6. New firefighters learn through "live fire training drills." In this simulated learning experience, a fire department acquires a building that is scheduled for demolition and sets it on fire for a controlled burn. With expert trainers on all sides, the trainee enters the building and practices fire-fighting skills while no lives are at risk (the simulation is managed by experts). This gives the firefighter invaluable experience that replicates the real thing.

7. To make your way into the glamorous (?) life of a Las Vegas blackjack dealer, you must first attend a dealer school. Currently there are five such schools in Las Vegas teaching students the ins and outs of games like blackjack, poker, roulette and craps. Of course, the games themselves can be learned through videos and books. But each student spends hours and hours perfecting their shuffling and dealing skills under the watchful eyes of a coach in a dealer practice room. There is no substitute for these hours of practice in order to reach the high-paying opportunities in the ritziest casinos of Vegas.

8. Throughout the complex process of mastering hairdressing, barbering, and cosmetology, most students will practice hair styling on a professional mannequin head. Subsequent to this initial practice tool, students (in "beauty school") will offer deeply discounted haircuts so that the student can continue to practice hair cutting under the skillful eye of the instructor. After all, would you get your hair styled by someone who had only completed a course of study online?

9. Law enforcement firearms training involves a weapon, live ammo, targets, and a protected area for shooting. This training is closely supervised with multiple protocols for safety. And yet, the best instructors create a realistic simulation of real life in order for the student to apply the training when needed. All the instructor

and trainer need to do in order to collect instant feedback is to look at the target after firing!

This is just a short list of industries and professions that count on their training being flawless. I have written all of these examples for you because you must know without doubt that this methodology is the only way to assure that your students are making progress, increasing buy in, and develop proficiency. If you're uncertain about all this and are confronted by a student who offers an objection, dismisses this approach, or reacts negatively, I assure you that your skills as a teacher and as a leader will atrophy if you decide to compromise your approach, that is, if you decide to appease the complaining student.

Why wouldn't you want your training to be effective? Too many people are willing to complain about poor performance instead of doing something to influence a difference. The ORBiT method is written to make sure that you get results, influence behavior, and enjoy the results you need. My expectation is that if you're going to invest your time in training and development, it will be time well spent and you can easily see the return on that investment of time. But behavior change isn't easy, and creating simulations for your use is going to require that you are absolutely convinced of their effectiveness. Otherwise, you should put this book down and pass it on to someone else.

Still reading? Wonderful. Then let's continue.

Adult students need to "try it out" for themselves. Once they can see, hear, and feel the information they are able to engage fully, validate the information for themselves, and then learn the new skills. Every quality training experience considers this reality and creates that interaction. As the teacher, you'll have to plan for this in advance and develop a simulation that involves the student in the process.

But let's go a little further. This step in the process is called "negative simulation." Strategically, the first use of simulation should be you, the trainer, simulating negative behaviors for your student to experience. Our overall goal in the first three steps of ORBiT is to secure a buy in. Demonstrating a negative simulation allows the student to see and experience the wrong behaviors in the interest of having them agree, "That was bad!"

So, this is what you do: In preparation for your training, consider what it is that you're intending to teach. Once you're clear on the content, you must develop a simulation that depicts the *opposite* behaviors. You must create an experience to show what you *don't* want—and the negative consequences that occur as a result. This is actually easier than it sounds.

Most of my clients request sales training and so I do it frequently. One concept that we teach in sales training is the need for the salesperson to be an effective listener. When it is time for a negative simulation of this concept, I create a simulation in which my trainee is the person I am selling to, and I am the salesperson. Rather than engaging in a two-way dialog in my simulated "sale," I (the salesperson) do all the talking.

It's easy for me to create (actually "recreate") this negative simulation. One of the first sales calls I ever made in my new company years ago was with the president of a local bank. I was so excited—and so nervous! He was a quiet, reserved man, and that only added to my nervousness. Once I got into his office I began a complex and lengthy presentation of my company, our programs, and products. On and on I rambled, growing louder and more elaborate in my explanations. After 25 minutes he spoke his first words, "Thank you for coming by, it was nice to meet you."

And that was that.

When I want to create a negative simulation that helps me make the point about effective listening in a sales call, all I have to do is recreate that experience—putting my trainee in the position of that bank President—and then it is easy for my trainee to experience the *opposite* of what they should do. The trainee can see, feel, hear, and experience the consequences of my negative behavior.

The challenge for us as trainers is to find a meaningful simulation no matter what we are training.

EMOTION

When I'm training someone, and I get to this step in my process, I literally want the student to feel an emotion that confirms the negative nature of what I've done. That emotion could be humor, outrage, frustration, or concern. But the power in this training step is in eliciting the emotion. Your role here is to construct a simulation, which allows your trainee to experience the negative result of doing something the wrong way. Here are some examples.

A. Let's go back to the airplane simulator. The training methodology does not consist of having the trainee fly a plane on autopilot while mimicking a two-hour flight from Atlanta to Boston. Rather, the simulator instructor introduces the student to a series of bad circumstances: wind shear, ice on the wings, losing hydraulics, etc. All of these are designed for the student to understand what happens when he doesn't successfully read the instrument panel, the radar, or pay attention to other system alerts.

"When you fail to check the indicator light, you won't notice the ice buildup on the wings. When you miss that, you'll lose flight controls and the results are disastrous." The simulator accurately "punishes" the trainee by simulating the failure. This entire exercise serves to create an emotional reaction to the negative behaviors, further convincing the trainee that what they did (or failed to do) was bad!

B. Modern medical simulation technology is already widely used and continues to grow. These simulators accurately mimic the response when improper treatment or technique is used. If the student applies proper technique the simulator responds with healthy "vital signs." Improper technique results in trauma.

This step may be the most difficult for the trainer.

This step may have the most impact on the learning.

This step requires preparation on your part.

This step significantly increases your student's buy-in.

Keep this in mind: the simulation does not need to be lengthy to be effective. The simulation needs to last just long enough to make your point. Once that has happened, end the simulation.

STUDENT=EXPERT

After the simulation is complete, it is vital that you debrief the student.

- What did you see?
- What did you experience?
- How did you feel?
- Did you like it? Why not?
- What suggestions would you make to improve your experience?

In this way the person you are training becomes the expert on the experience. This is a key element to successfully training adults. In order for adults to be engaged in the training, their experience and opinions must be involved. So we ask them to tell us what they think, what they liked, and how they evaluated the experience. You are seeking confirmation from the student about the negative simulation: that was bad, right? Getting that agreement is crucial in order for you to progress to step three: positive simulation. If you haven't created emotion around this negative simulation you may be reducing the overall impact of your training.

Negative simulation is one aspect of the ORBiT process that is different from many development processes. Use it to your advantage. If you've done this properly, the student has experienced a negative emotion. Extract that feeling. Encourage them to talk about it. I can promise that your trainees do have opinions about the process you are teaching. When asking them to share those opinions, they are the experts on those feelings. This dialog can create a wonderful collaborative environment for the continuation of your training.

You want their opinions. You want their contribution. You want them to be involved.

One of the reasons that training adults sometimes feels demeaning is that the trainer treats the students as if they are school students. Here, at this point in the ORBiT process, the student is the expert. They've just had a negative experience. Let them tell you about it.

I was training a group of sales reps in the outdoor sports industry a few years ago. The focus was on elevating the in-store experience so that their clients would differentiate their brand from others in a positive way. I did two demonstrations.

First, I had two of the reps walk up to a counter as if they were walking into a restaurant seeking a table. I acted as if I was a typical host at a typical restaurant.

"Good evening," I said. "Table for two?"

My students, said, "Yes, please."

"Right this way."

I grabbed two "menus" and walked them to a table and said, "Here are your menus, Robert will be right with you." And then walked off.

I ended the simulation by asking the two of them:

"What type of restaurant is this?" they both answered, "A restaurant chain. Mid-level."

I continued, "How much money does that host earn for his job?" My trainees responded, "Minimum wage."

Finally, I asked, "How much are you expecting to pay for the meal?" They smiled and said, "Not much. It's going to be basic fare."

"Good. Thanks, I agree. Nothing wrong with what happened, but that is all you expect from that greeting, right?"

I then reset the simulation and asked the same two people to walk up to a counter and ask for a table. I forecasted that this would be a different restaurant.

"Good evening, folks. My name is Dan. Welcome to The Grove."

My trainees looked shocked, but they responded with big smiles and said, "Thank you!"

I continued, "Do you have a reservation with us this evening?"
"No." They replied flatly.

I smiled and folded my hands together, "That will be no problem, we have plenty of seating. I have a nice booth along the far wall, or I can seat you by the window with a beautiful view of our garden. Which do you prefer?"

The students looked at each other—and they were getting into the acting by now—one said to the other, "I don't care, honey, what do you prefer?" (Since they were co-workers and not a couple, the other students laughed at this.)

Finally, one of them said, "We'll take the view."

"Marvelous," I said. "Please follow me."

As I "seated" them at the table I said, "Robert will be your server tonight. He is one of our finest. But I will also check in with you to make sure you are well cared for. By the way, are the two of you celebrating anything special tonight?"

Because my trainees were fully playing along now, one of them smiled and said, "It's our anniversary!"

Continuing, I smiled and said, "Congratulations. I will alert the kitchen right away."

I ended the simulation by asking the students, "What type of restaurant is this?" They answered, "A very nice place. Probably locally owned." Next question: "How much money is this person earning?" They both answered, "He's probably the owner. If not, he's a well-paid maître d'."

I finished with, "How much are you expecting to pay for this meal?" Both smiled and said, "This one is going to be expensive."

I pressed on with the entire group: "What was the difference between the two experiences?"

I received numerous great answers from the group:

- Night and day. The second one was much more valuable!
- The second person wasn't just a host. He took ownership.
- The first one was just doing a job. No sense of ownership.
- The second person acted like he cared about our experience.

By asking these questions in this way, I made my trainees *the experts!* They had just experienced the simulation. They had opinions. They were able to contribute. They could see, feel, and hear it for themselves. By asking them to share their opinions, the teaching and the application of my point was being delivered by the students themselves. They were the experts. This level of involvement creates a dynamic learning environment. People are alert, engaged, and they participate. It will set the tone for powerful learning and grateful students.

CHAPTER FOUR

Shift Happens

POSITIVE SIMULATION

Once you have firmly established what the *negative* behavior is—and confirmed with your trainee that he or she agrees with you—there is a void, which is then filled by the curious student who asks, "So, if that was the wrong way, then what is the right way?"

This is a powerful moment in the training process. It's like an unresolved chord in a song. This creates dissonance, which is a technique used for centuries by musicians to keep the audience engaged, surprised, and emotionally involved.

Dissonance, resolution, and suspense are used to create musical interest. Where a melody or chord progression is expected to resolve to a certain note or chord, a different but similarly suitable note can be resolved to instead, creating an interesting and unexpected sound. For example, the deceptive cadence. The negative simulation sets the tone of dissonance. Now it is time to resolve this unresolved issue by demonstrating the correct process: a positive simulation.

"Cognitive dissonance refers to a situation involving conflicting attitudes, beliefs or behaviors. This produces a feeling of discomfort leading to an alteration in one of the attitudes, beliefs or behaviors to reduce the discomfort and restore balance etc." Saul McLeod, *Simply Psychology*

If you've created a realistic negative simulation your student should be experience some internal conflict:

- I always thought that method was best. But now that I've experienced it, I realize I was wrong.
- I never knew what it felt like on this side of the experience.
- I'm going to have to change the way I do things.
- I'd like to know a better way.

"Leon Festinger, in 1957, proposed cognitive dissonance theory, which states that a powerful motive to maintain cognitive consistency can give rise to irrational and sometimes maladaptive behavior. According to Festinger, we hold many ideas about the world and ourselves; when they clash, a discrepancy is evoked, resulting in a state of tension known as cognitive dissonance. As the experience of dissonance is unpleasant, we are motivated to reduce or eliminate it, and achieve consonance (i.e., agreement)." Saul McLeod, *Simply Psychology*

Into this void you will demonstrate a better way.

Into this unresolved conflict of attitudes you will supply a solution.

Into this dissonance you will create order.

You do this by creating a compelling *positive* simulation of the correct behaviors.

SIMULATE POSITIVE BEHAVIOR: LET THE STUDENT EXPERIENCE IT

We have now arrived at the point where many trainers begin: show the trainee what you want them to do. You can see that the ORBiT method takes a much different (and longer) approach. If you start here—without context or a negative simulation—the trainee may not be fully engaged and ready to learn.

But because you have established context and conducted a negative simulation, your trainee understands why we're doing this exercise and is anxious to learn the best way to do it. So, you will create a simulation (again, involving your trainee) in which you will show your trainee exactly what you want him to do: a positive simulation.

In order to create a realistic simulation, you, the trainer, will have to immerse yourself in a role. You are literally showing your trainee what you want them to do once the training is complete. Conducting this positive simulation involves many actions that occur at the same time:

- You are carefully exhibiting the correct behaviors
- Your trainee is participating along with you in the simulation
- Your trainee will be able to evaluate this experience--they are on the receiving end
- Your trainees can validate for themselves that this approach is best
- Your trainee can see it, feel it, hear it and touch it. This is totally immersive

This is a vital part of the learning/development process. After all, it is difficult to do something if you can't first envision it. Your proper demonstration of the correct action helps the student create the mental template for what they should do.

If you've ever watched a golf tournament you've seen this very action. Professional golfers go through this sequence:

- The golfer approaches the tee box
- The golfer puts the tee and ball in the ground
- The golfer stands behind the golf ball and looks down the fairway
- The golfer intently stares at the place where she intends to hit the ball

- After several moments of this, the golfer approaches the ball, gets into position, and then drives the ball down the fairway.

What is the golfer doing as she stands behind the ball? She is imagining her shot. She is literally picturing exactly where she wants it to go. This mental discipline has proven to be vital to golf success. One cannot physically perform the skill until it can be performed mentally.

> "Brain studies now reveal that thoughts produce the same mental instructions as actions. Mental imagery impacts many cognitive processes in the brain: motor control, attention, perception, planning, and memory. So the brain is getting trained for actual performance during visualization. It's been found that mental practices can enhance motivation, increase confidence and self-efficacy, improve motor performance, prime your brain for success, and increase states of flow—all relevant to achieving your best life!"
> —AJ LeVan, *Psychology Today*, December 3, 2009

By producing a positive demonstration of the behaviors you want, your trainees can more easily picture this for themselves. This mental imagery is literally the first step in your students' ability to perform properly.

You may have seen one of many communication "games" that are often used in team building exercises at corporate retreats or seminars. The exercise goes something like this:

Two people are selected. They are asked to sit back to back, in such a way that neither can see the other. Each of them is given a piece of paper. One of them is also given a pencil. One of the participants has a page with some sort of drawing on it. The other participant (the one with the pencil) has a blank sheet of paper. Got it?

Now for the fun part. The person who has the page with the drawing proceeds to describe the drawing in such a way that the other person can duplicate the drawing by only following their partner's instruction. There are, of course, some rules, but the premise is simple. It is very difficult for someone to perfectly replicate a drawing without first seeing it. No matter how good of a communicator the "describer" is, the person who draws just can't seem to picture the original. What is most likely is the person drawing begins to reference some other image from their past. The mental images that he already possesses actually prevent him from properly hearing the instruction and completing the task properly. When I've seen this exercise performed, I've never seen anyone get close to the original.

The good news for us—in the ORBiT process—is we aren't playing any games. No guessing is required. You will take the time to actually show your student want you want. Imagine how easy it would be for those poor volunteers who are sitting back to back in this drawing game if one person could just show the other their drawing. "Here it is. Look at this and then copy it!"

That's what you are doing in this phase of ORBiT: "Here, look at this and then copy it."

You will be helping your student see, imagine, and visualize. This is a major step in preparing to learn.

AH-HA!

What your trainee will see in this positive simulation should be in stark contrast to what they saw in the negative simulation. Once they see the ideal behaviors you want them to experience a paradigm shift.

Paradigm shift: a fundamental change in approach or underlying assumptions.

In teaching, I *love* creating paradigm shifts. Your training can be so powerful when your student can instantly change the way they look at something—and *never* see it the same way again. Take a look at the list below. Have you seen the hidden meaning in these logos? Once you've seen them you can never unsee them! If you have never taken the time to look closely at these logos, step away for a minute and enjoy the power of a new paradigm shift!

- FedEx Logo (an arrow is hidden in the empty space between the E and the X)
- Tour De France Logo (a cyclist is riding a bike made out of the O and the Yellow Sun)
- Amazon Logo (look for "A to Z with a smile")
- Toblerone (can you find a bear in the mountain?)

For our purposes the paradigm shift experience can be very powerful. If you've created the right two simulations (negative followed by positive) your student is possibly experiencing a new way of looking at something. You may be addressing a fundamental point of view that they have held for many years. This "Ah-Ha" moment can be life changing.

When I first started mountain biking I fell in love with the sport immediately. Even though I was riding three or four times a week there was one technique that was consistently causing me to fall: I could not ride over a log that was more than a few inches high. Unfortunately, since I was learning the sport in central Illinois, one of the primary features of mountain bike trails in central Illinois was the placing of logs in a number of areas along the trail. I just could not figure it out. So, I either attempted to increase my speed (which caused many epic fails) or I dismounted and walked my bike over the obstacle.

One weekend I decided to participate in a trail building event at a local mountain bike trail. At the end of the day, the group (20+ mountain bikers) rode the trail together. In order not to face embarrassment, I strategically moved to the back of the pack, so that no one could see me walk my bike over the multiple logs that I knew were on the trail. The head of the IMBA trail building crew, Mark Schmidt got there first.

"Go ahead, Mark, I'll bring up the rear."

He wouldn't hear of it.

"Nope," he said, "I'll be the last rider in. That's my job."

Well, this disrupted my plan. Seeing no way around the inevitable I started the ride. Slowly. I slowed some more.

"Don't you want to go around me, Mark?" I asked.

"I'm fine, " Mark replied. Why was he so nice?

As we approached the first log, the main group was nowhere in sight. (Relief.) Unfortunately, Mark was right behind me. Resigning myself to my fate, I stopped and got off my bike.

"What's wrong?" Mark asked.

So I told him. "I can't ride my bike over obstacles."

Mark smiled, "Most of us can't when we start riding. Let me see what you're doing."

So, I backed up and rode up to the log, giving it my best effort. Of course, I fell.

Mark asked me to stand beside the log. He told me that he was going to show me what I was doing. "Pay close attention to where my weight is. I'm going to do what you are doing and you should see the problem."

As he approached the log, he leaned way back and pulled up on the handlebars, which created the exact fall I had just produced.

"You see" he said, "You're leaning back and losing your balance."

Mark then carefully walked me through the process of riding a bike over a log:

- As you approach, lift the front wheel onto the log while pushing down on your front pedal
- Once your tire is over the log, shift your weight forward allowing your rear tire to lift up and over the log
- Unweight the handlebar, which will allow you to smoothly roll off the log completely

Guess what? It made sense! I immediately wanted to try it. Once I had watched him do it properly, I could clearly understand the difference between what I had been doing versus what I should have been doing. I backed up down the trail and approached the log. Using my newfound process I easily crossed the log—and every other log on the trail that day. In fact, I have never had trouble crossing logs since. Once I saw it done the correct way, I experienced a paradigm shift and that propelled me to instant success.

POP QUIZ
A short test given to students without prior warning.

Thinking back to my days as an Alabama schoolteacher, no words brought more angst, more horror or more reaction than these, "Please take out your pencils and a piece of paper, and number from one to ten. We're going to have a pop quiz."

I can still hear their cries in my mind, "No, please, stop this madness!"

From the perspective of those students a pop quiz was some form of retribution for poor attention or bad behavior. But, truly, all I wanted to do was find out how much of the class they had retained. The pop quiz had very little to do with their final grade, it didn't count for much in the average. But it gave me, the teacher, valuable immediate feedback.

- Did the students "get it"?
- Were they paying attention?
- Did they grasp the key concepts?
- Could they communicate it back to me accurately?

Once I knew this I could take the next logical steps. If the class had a good grasp of the material, I could move on with confidence and know that we were making progress. If, however, the students failed the pop quiz, I had to change my course direction, slow down and revisit the material I had just presented. They didn't understand yet. I couldn't proceed.

In the chronology of ORBiT, look at what has happened:

1. You established the *context* for why you are conducting this training

2. You demonstrated the *negative* behavior that doesn't work— and confirmed that with the trainee.

3. You showed the *positive* behavior that you want.

So, at this crucial moment, you need to make sure your student saw this positive behavior. The student needs to be able to restate it to you. The student should communicate a clear understanding of what you did, how you did it, and why you did it—and confirm that they agree with your approach. Your debrief (pop quiz) could sound like this:

"What did you see me do?"

"Where was I during the simulation?"

"And then what did I do?"

"What did you think of that?"

"How did you feel as you experienced this behavior?"

Let me take you back to the day I first taught my sons how to use the lawn mower. After demonstrating the dangers of the machine and showing them the proper operation of the mower, I conducted a short pop quiz to make sure that they understood everything they had just seen.

Me: "So, what are the first steps you take prior to mowing a section of the yard?"

Sons: "You walk through the yard and remove any sticks, rocks, dog bones, or toys."

Me: "Why?"

Sons: "If the blade hits any of those things it could discharge into someone and hurt them."

Me: "What does this safety bar do?"

Sons: "It shuts off the mower once you let go of the handle."

Me: "Why is that important?"

Sons: "No one should be on the side of the mower while it is running"

Me: "Why not?"

Sons: "The blade is dangerous and could cut your hands or feet—or discharge a rock."

Of course this exchange seems elementary, but with so much at risk it was crucial that they understood the risk and that *I* knew that they understood the risk.

Your use of the pop quiz, of course, would be appropriate to the topic as well as the trainee you are working with. But don't leave the positive simulation phase of training until your student can tell you what they learned.

Why? If you look ahead at the ORBiT process, what is coming next? Demonstration.

Next up, your student will be required to show you the proper behavior. In order for them to correctly replicate the actions you're looking for, you should confirm that they have identified them in advance.

MOST IMPORTANT OF ALL: ALIGNMENT

Certainly the danger in bypassing this step is moving forward with the assumption that learning (and a buy in) has taken place. I have learned over the years that assuming is the enemy of learning progress.

Picture this:

A college student approaches his father with a request. He wants to borrow his father's car so that he and his friends can go on spring break. His father considers his son's plea and offers a response, "I'll let you guys borrow my car, but I want to speak with all of you before you leave." His son was elated. "This is going to be great!" He tells his friends, "We just need to chat with my Dad before we leave and we're all set."

The day for spring break departure arrived. Dad gathers his son and his two friends and says simply, "You boys have a great spring break. I'm happy to loan you my car. But remember this—and this is very important: You can't put too much oil in this car."

The boys looked at each other and nodded. "Got it. You can't put too much oil in this car."

Dad bids them farewell, and off they go, headed for the sunny skies of spring break.

The son, who is driving, pulls off the highway at the first exit and stops into a gas station. One of his friends asks, "What are you doing?"

The son says, "I'm stopping to get oil. You heard my father. He said 'you can't put too much oil in this car;' so I'm going to make sure we have lots of oil—after all, it's impossible to overfill it. We need to keep a lot of oil with us."

"No," says the first friend. "Your Father meant that you should not put a lot of oil in the car. I would recommend that we never put any oil in it!"

The second friend chimes in, "You are both wrong. Your father meant that *you* should not put oil in the car. We should add oil, but we need a mechanic to add the oil for us. *We* should not be doing it at all."

The Dad, the son, and both friends all heard the same request. Each one interpreted it differently. In one meaning they're adding lots of oil; in another meaning they're not adding any oil. Here's a perfect example of why it's important to check and double check to insure that your communication is clear and that you and your trainee understand things exactly the same way.

As you approach the end of the first three steps of ORBiT and turn your attention to the next three steps, you must insure that you have achieved one primary goal: alignment. Let's go to the dictionary: Alignment: a state of agreement or cooperation among persons, groups, nations, etc., with a common cause or viewpoint.

During my years training adults I have learned one truth: Training adults is less about learning how and more about getting an agreement on *why*. So the first three steps in our process are designed to secure agreement, and to make sure that you and your trainee are on the same page.

If this isn't the case, if there's misalignment, your remaining three steps will be ineffective.

CHAPTER FIVE

Skills + Alignment = Performance

DEMONSTRATION

The only way that the trainer can know that the student has learned a particular skill or process is to have them demonstrate it. It's only in this demonstration that the teacher can see what progress has been made. Teachers who don't insist on a demonstration component in their process are risking some very serious breakdowns in the student's development.

Allow your trainee to put their new knowledge into practice. This is fundamental to all levels of learning. Of course, some learners are uncomfortable with this part of the development process because they may feel unprepared. They may feel conspicuous. They may have never worked this way before. There is a reason that the number one fear in most people is the fear of public speaking. When one is at the front of the room, with an audience, you are exposed, vulnerable. Mistakes are magnified. What if I mess up? What if I don't do it well? These fears may cause your student to pause, or even offer excuses as to why they cannot or will not participate. You must be firm, reassuring, respectful, and empathetic. But if you intend to change behavior, you must press on.

I prefer to act as if it is the next logical step in the process. "Ok, Bill, let's have you try it now" or "Ok, Bill, let's switch roles." Or, "Ok,

Bill, your turn." No big deal, just step up and get started! But there could be serious reasons why your student doesn't want to demonstrate the behaviors your teaching:

- They don't agree with the approach and haven't told you yet
- They still don't understand or are uncertain about what to do
- They don't have the skills necessary to execute, because they've never done this before
- They are fearful of failure

Ultimately, the reason why will become obvious. In fact, that is why we must proceed. Observing his behavior during the demonstration will tell you everything you need to know in order to help your trainee learn, develop, and master their new skills. It is, in fact, The Moment of Truth. *Show me.* Simple words, but a powerful moment in learning. Up until now in the ORBiT process the trainer has been doing all the "heavy lifting". Now you turn your attention to the student.

"You try it."

"Let me see you do it."

"Your turn!"

"Why don't you see if you can do it?"

"Show me."

Throughout your training session your student may have been giving you signals that they "get it":

- Head nods
- Thumbs up
- Comments of agreement
- Answering positively when you ask, "Do you understand?"

I've learned through raising four children that just because one of them tells me, "Yes, I understand", that is no guarantee they do. So I have learned to regularly use this phrase: "Show me."

Why is this the moment of truth? Because your student will, for the first time, be expected to perform. There will be no hiding from the truth. Is he "on board"? Is he capable of demonstrating the skills you've been teaching? Is he engaged in the learning exercise? Has he been paying attention?

There is a mentoring formula I have been aware of and used all of my life:

- I do, you watch
- I do, you help
- You do, I help
- You do, I watch

Unfortunately, there are so many different versions of this I'm not sure who to credit with the original other than to say that I know it wasn't me! But according to this formula, we have arrived at the final step: *You do, I watch*. And this is why it is the moment of truth.

Here's how you create it:

Using the same situation you have been using in steps two (negative simulation) and three (positive simulation) you will switch roles with your trainee and your trainee will now demonstrate the correct behaviors you have just shown in the positive simulation.

A. You are participating in the simulation in order to create realism.

B. No surprises. Follow the same situation you had in steps two and three.

C. The student has to implement the behaviors you've just demonstrated. It is necessary that they think on their feet.

D. While you are participating in this simulation you must also watch the student's performance in order to evaluate it.

E. It can be challenging to keep up with everything that is happening. After all, you're serving at least three roles:

Simulation participant (to some degree, an actor).

Coach; watching the performance to evaluate it.

Director of the simulation: timekeeper (setting it up, when to start, when to stop).

For 50 years Harry Parker was the head coach of the Harvard rowing program. He may well have been the winningest coach of any sport ever. He led his teams to 22 undefeated seasons and 16 national titles. He coached six Olympic teams, winning three medals. During his years he coached 52 collegiate athletes who went on to become Olympians. His coaching style was very interactive. As the eight-man rowing teams rowed, he would be piloting a motorboat right beside the crew. Picture this: He spoke to his team through an old-school megaphone. Gently offering encouragement, tips, and instruction. He wasn't a shouter. He didn't threaten. The crewmembers were demonstrating the actions. He was right there watching. Evaluating. Coaching and directing the team. This wasn't the race—this was the practice. The crew demonstrated the behavior for him to watch and improve. That simple model worked for Harvard for half a century. It's the right model for you, too.

Show me. *Let me see you do it.*

Once the student performs the demonstration, you will either see a poor performance or a good performance.

If the student exhibits a poor performance, there are two possible causes:

1. No Alignment
2. Poor skills

NO ALIGNMENT = POOR DEMONSTRATION

The fourth step in ORBiT is crucial. We ask our trainee to demonstrate back to us what we have taught. Now, it is possible for them to get away with deceiving you with remarks like: "Yes, I agree" or "You are all over it" or "This is great. I love it!" But once we ask them to *demonstrate* this new skill for us to observe, you can count on this: If they don't agree with us in theory, they will not demonstrate it successfully. Worse, if they're not aligned with you philosophically, they will either refuse to demonstrate at all, or they will perform badly during the demonstration.

After all, you are asking your student to perform a task, action or process. The student must believe this task, action, or process is absolutely in alignment with their values, beliefs, and opinions. The behavior and the student's belief system *must* be aligned.

Some years ago I was in a training session for a retail client who sells ski equipment and service. We held our meeting with some of his key sales staff in the back of his store before store hours. I was teaching a simple principle: when customers enter the store, avoid asking, "May I help you." Instead, simply greet your customer and welcome them to your store. Using the ORBiT method, I did several demonstrations of this process. I showed some of the negative experiences associated with greeting customers—and got agreement from most of the staff that these experiences were indeed negative. Then I demonstrated the positive simulation and dialoged with the class about why that was better.

Throughout the early part of my training exercise, I watched one member of the staff—I'll call him Ray—who was not buying in.

- He sat at the back of the room
- He made sure he was hidden (he sat behind someone who obscured my view of him)
- He whispered to his neighbor and laughed at some of my points
- Several times he left the training to "use the rest room" or "make a phone call"

And yet, whenever I asked the members of the class to tell me if they disagreed or had concerns, he never spoke up. I would frequently check in with comments like "So what do you think?" and "Are we on board so far?" and "What do you folks think of this approach?"

As a trainer, I've learned the lack of response does not equate to alignment!

So, I began to bring members of the class to the front of the room. Using the simulation I had created I asked the students to *show me*. One by one they did. Of course some students struggled, but most did the demonstration and had fun with it. Collectively we laughed and enjoyed the process of becoming comfortable with a new skill. Then it was Ray's turn.

Ray reluctantly walked to the front of the class. We began the simulation (he was to greet a "customer" in some other way besides, "May I help you?") He struggled. In fact everyone in the room could see his discomfort. He shuffled his feet. He turned away from me. He was frustrated within the simulation and did not do it well. Finally, he shouted in desperation, "This is stupid."

"What's stupid about it, Ray?" I asked.

"I don't like role playing. I already know what I'm doing and I don't want to do this." He was indignant.

"But I haven't seen you do this the way we discussed." I gently pressed forward.

"Yeah, well, I don't see any problem with asking 'May I help you.' It's worked for me for three years and I see no reason to change now."

There! Now we have the real issue on the table. He did not agree with the method. Because of that, he was unwilling and even unable to perform the process I was asking for.

If you and your student are not aligned philosophically, your student will not successfully demonstrate the new skill.

POOR SKILLS = POOR DEMONSTRATION

There is another, more common reason for a poor demonstration: The student doesn't possess the necessary skills.

As you have progressed through your previous three steps (context, negative and positive simulation), it is very likely that your student has been introduced to something new. This could be the first time she has seen this new behavior. As the teacher, it's important for you to recognize this reality and respond accordingly. When you see a poor demonstration—and confirm that it is not due to a lack of alignment—your real teaching begins. So your initial reaction is crucial. Recognize that this information or behavior is something that the student still needs to learn. Be patient and work to develop the skill.

Kindergarten teachers have always inspired me. You'll find them to be among the most educated members of the school system: masters degrees, board certification, and continued education credits. With all that education, what do they spend their time doing? Playing games, handing out milk, reading stories. You won't see these teachers standing behind a podium in front of a PowerPoint presentation, saying things like, "Today, students we will be introducing the Vowel, "A" which is from the Greek alpha. It is a derivative of the Phoenician letter aleph... Johnny, take that straw out of Billy's ear!"

No, you would be more likely to see a kindergarten teacher kneeling or sitting on a small stool at eye level. She's holding up an inflatable letter A ("Mrs. Achoo!"). She's almost whispering, "Boys and girls, look who is visiting us today. It's Mrs. A! Can you look around our classroom and see Mrs. A anywhere else in our room?"

That's because, even though the teacher is highly educated, she must meet the students at *their* level of skill. This is likely to be the situation with the adults you work with. They're going to be unable to demonstrate these new behaviors simply because they don't possess the skills to do so.

Since 1977, I have taught hundreds of students how to play guitar. The reality of "Poor Skills=Poor Demonstration" is clearly seen in the early days of learning how to play. Typically, the student has spent hours listening to and watching guitarists play. Thinking to themselves, "This can't be that hard," they borrow or buy their first guitar. Certainly, they have dreamed big dreams of performing for friends around a campfire or thrilling thousands of fans in arenas around the world. And then they wrap their untrained fingers around the neck of the guitar and place their fingers on the fret board for the first time. Reality. Their fingers simply will not do what they are supposed to do. If you've never played guitar, I can tell you that this is the most awkward position for your fingers to be in. New muscles are put into use: muscles that are not frequently used. Add to that frustration the pain associated with pressing and holding a bronze wound guitar string and many guitar students walk away from the instrument in the first month. Over time, skilled guitarists develop calluses, which help reduce the pain. New guitarists are still experiencing this for the first time. They don't have the skills. They aren't used to these muscles being used. They have tender fingertips. They cannot perform well because *they don't possess the skills.*

This is where the student starts the learning process. Tender. New muscles. Unrehearsed. But with patience, reinforcement, coaching and feedback, students who want to learn can develop these muscles, "toughen the fingertips," and develop the skills you are looking to improve.

SKILL + ALIGNMENT = PERFORMANCE

The sign of progress to this point is a successful demonstration by your trainee. You want to see the appropriate level of skill being demonstrated during this section. This is only possible for your trainee *if* they agree with you in theory *and* if they possess the skills to perform. These are two rather substantial if's. I have previously stated that adults learn and change behavior in a different way than school children do. Adults must see the need for change. Adults must agree with the approach. Adults want to try it out for themselves. Adults want their experiences and opinions considered during the training. If your student does not buy in to your approach they will not successfully demonstrate the action. If your student does not possess the skill they cannot demonstrate the action.

So, this point in our process is vital. Here you will confirm:

- My student is on board. Bought in. Aligned.
- My student possesses the skills to demonstrate the new behaviors. Competence.

Alignment is such a powerful, important word in business. If you search out all the ways the word alignment is used you'll see it is widespread. Politics, automobile tires, Dungeons and Dragons, golf, chiropractic medicine, word processing, yoga, astronomy, football, graphic design, and the list goes on and on. Its meaning is simple: to fall into line—to come to agreement. We're "on the same page," as the expression goes.

I grew up in the Deep South, so therefore I spent many Sundays sitting in a pew in a country church. An important part of the service was singing hymns. So we all used hymnals that were provided in the pews. It was common in those days that these small, poor country churches didn't have enough songbooks to go around and so they would frequently have multiple versions of songbooks scattered throughout the church. When the song leader announced the next hymn we were to sing, it might sound like this:

"Please turn to page 65 in the red hymnal, page 178 in the blue hymnal, and page 432 in the green hymnal." Even though we were singing from different hymnals we were all looking at the same song: "Onward Christian Soldiers." In that way, we were all on the same page. In order for the church to be in unison during the singing of the hymns the pastor had to arrange for all church members to get on the same page. The result was beautiful music! Harmony! Unity! Training adults, then, is as much about getting everyone on the same page as it is about developing skills. This step in ORBiT confirms that you have been successful at both.

DUCKS IN A ROW

If you're focused on changing adult behavior, this is an important "mile marker." Confirm that you're seeing the skills you want *and* the alignment you need to move forward. One could say that you are getting all your "ducks in a row." When I began looking for the origin of this phrase, I was surprised to see that there are multiple possibilities for how this phrase came to be. Some have said that this term came from the sport of Duckpin bowling. The bowling pins are often called "ducks." Prior to the advent of automated pinsetter machines there was a designated pinsetter—or pinspotter, whose job it was to correctly set all the "ducks in a row." In other words, put everything in its proper place before the game could be played correctly.

Others have advocated that the term came from the classic carnival game, "Duck Shoot." In this children's game, found at carnivals, players use a toy pistol to shoot mechanical ducks that are rolling by at a slow place. To be successful means that the player shot all of the "ducks in a row." The meaning here is similar: everything is being done properly and according to plan.

I've even read an explanation that the term comes from the familiar image of ducks, flying south in a "V" pattern. To effectively fly in groups—and maximize their energy—ducks fly in a pattern (literally, "ducks in a row"), which allows them to take advantage of each duck's effort for the benefit of the group. The meaning is clear: aligned flight saves energy, reduces obstacles, and advances the cause faster and easier.

My use of the phrase is much simpler than that. I lived for several years in Memphis, Tennessee, home to the iconic Peabody Hotel. If you've been to the hotel, you already know the story I'm going to tell. In the center of the grand lobby is a large fountain. In the fountain are five North American mallards. They swim and play all day and guests enjoy watching their activity and interact with them. At 5:00 a red carpet is rolled out and the "Duck Master" calls for the ducks to prepare to leave. The drake leads the other ducks in a delightful walk from the fountain to the elevator, where they are taken to their rooftop home. Watching these ducks follow each other is reminiscent of the way you would always picture a mother duck leading her young: all in single file, one behind the other. If one is out of place, she can identify it and react quickly. For convenience, safety and efficiency, she keeps all her "ducks in a row."

Changing behavior is a process. As the leader of this process, you are looking for progress and demonstration in two areas right here:

- Your student is beginning to demonstrate the skills needed for the behaviors you're looking for *and*

- Your student agrees with the approach, philosophy, and ratio-
  nale for these behaviors.

This alignment creates momentum, progress, and energy toward the goal. All of your ducks are in a row!

COACH OBSERVES AND EVALUATES

Even before writing this book, I have taught ORBiT for well over a
decade. I have always stated that the second step, negative simulation, is the most difficult step to execute in the ORBiT process. I have
felt that because few of us understand the impact it has on the final
outcome, and most of us don't think about doing something badly
(even in a simulation).

I've had a paradigm shift in past few months. One of my
long-time clients, Tom Henry, along with his brother, Peter, owns
Landry's Bikes in Boston. Tom and his team have been integrating
the ORBiT process among his store managers. After spending six
months with this method, he and his managers all agreed: the step
that makes the most impact is also the step that is the most difficult
to implement. Here it is: the coach observes and evaluates. The effective coach is able to *observe* the behavior of his or her trainee,
evaluate it to identify where the opportunity is for improvement,
and *formulate* this evaluation into effective feedback, delivered to
the student. This is not easy. This unique skill is what characterizes
any professional.

In Weaverville, North Carolina, we call Danny Fender "The
Tire Whisperer." He owns Fender Tire and may well be one of the
most modest, hard-working men you'll ever meet. My partner, Leslie, was teaching her 15-year-old daughter Makenzie how to drive
during her one-year temporary permit process. As often happens
during those months, Makenzie slightly bumped the curb while
driving through a particularly complicated (and busy) stretch of
downtown Asheville. Mother and daughter were fine but shaken by

the experience. She called me and asked, "What should I do?" I replied, "Is the tire okay?" Leslie answered, "I think so, it's not flat." So I had her drive home.

Once she got home I looked over the tire and determined that "The Tire Whisperer" should probably look over it. I drove the car over to his place. Danny looked at the tire and within five seconds declared, "You'll need to replace this tire, the steel belt has been broken." After looking at millions of tires over the decades, Danny can spot an irregularity almost instantly. I've looked at a few tires in my day, too, but I couldn't see the problem. Therein lies the skill: observe and evaluate. This is what separates the amateur from the pro. To master your skill of influence, you'll have to pay particular attention to developing this ability. Observe and evaluate.

CHAPTER SIX

How Coach K earned a Tar Heel's respect

FEEDBACK

Feedback: /ˈfēd̩bak/ The return of a portion of the output of a process or system to the input, especially when used to maintain performance or to control a system or process.

All of the steps we have taken thus far have brought us to this very important moment. You and your trainee have agreed on the approach. They have participated as you showed them the negative behaviors and then again as you showed the positive behaviors. Then, when it was their turn, they attempted to replicate these positive behaviors. You have just watched their attempt. You know what you were looking for. But what did the trainee do? Did the performance match the expectation/standard? Now is the time for you to give feedback. The goal of feedback is to coach, correct, or reinforce. I have noticed over the years that many managers are reluctant to offer feedback. Here are some reasons why:

- They don't feel qualified to offer suggestions
- They fear that the feedback could lead to resentment from the student
- They aren't certain they know what to suggest
- They don't know how
- They question themselves ("Who am I to offer a critique?")

- They believe they must be an accomplished expert on the activity in order to coach it

Remember the (Gold Medal) 2012 US Olympic Basketball Team? LeBron James may well be the greatest basketball player to ever play the game. Standing next to him, at any Olympic basketball game, is Coach K, the famous Duke University Basketball coach and perennial Olympic "Dream Team" coach. Do you think Coach K is a better basketball player than LeBron James? Could he beat LeBron in a game of one-on-one? Was Coach K *ever* better than LeBron? No. In fact, Coach K didn't even play in the NBA. More to the point, that doesn't matter. Coach K is able to give feedback to LeBron because he is a great *coach*. He has perspective. He can see the game differently that LeBron can. He has insights and strategy.

Coaching the game is different than playing the game.

I've watched a lot of basketball in my life. Because I grew up in eastern North Carolina my college basketball allegiances were set early on. So, twice a week, I turned on the Jefferson Pilot Basketball Network and watched my Carolina Tar Heels battle their way through the tough ACC. But when I'm watching basketball I'm saying things like, "Look, we scored!" "Come on guys, catch up!" "Hey, that was a foul!" Because I watch the game like a fan watches the game, I get caught up in the emotion of it and I pay no attention to the specifics.

Krzyzewski watches the game like a tactician. This is what he's thinking about and looking out for:

- What defense is the opponent playing?
- Who is out of position?
- What play should we run based on what the defense is doing?
- Where is the weakness in the opponent's team that I can exploit?

He watches the game, then shouts instruction (feedback) to his players. He calls timeouts and communicates (feedback) his strategy to the team. Coach K doesn't watch the game like I watch the game!

This same principle is true in golf. Picture Jordan Spieth with his swing coach, Cameron McCormick. Cameron has never played a PGA tour event. He could not beat Jordan in a round of golf. And yet, he tells Jordan how to improve his game. He has something Jordan doesn't have: perspective. He's able to observe Jordan's swing and determine what's missing—and how it could be improved.

Your role as coach includes this simple process:

- Observe the student's behavior.
- Compare this behavior against the standard.
- Offer suggestions that will change the student's behavior to align with the standard.

In order to be effective at feedback you must know what you want. You must be able to identify the behaviors that will improve performance. This is why I'm not a golf coach. If I were Jordan Spieth's golf coach I wouldn't be able to help him. My "coaching" would sound something like this:

"Jordan, I noticed that when you hit the ball it sliced out of bounds to the right. Instead of that, you want to hit the ball straight down the fairway. So, next time, when you hit it, try to hit it straight. No slicing."

I know what the desired end result it. I just don't know *how* to get it. Jordan's coach—Cameron McCormick—does. That is because he focuses on activity, not results.

SELF-EVALUATION

One important way for a student to "lock in" the material is to do a self-evaluation of their performance. It is also a great way for you, the teacher, to discern how much progress the student has made.

Sadly, few people are able to be truthful with themselves. To be unbiased about oneself is probably not possible. In fact, in my research for this book, I was unable to find a word for it. The best way to say it seems to be this combination of words: unbiased self-judgment. I would suppose that the reason there's no word for it is because so few people possess the skill. It may be impossible to fairly evaluate yourself. Have you ever had to complete a self-evaluation form for an annual review? Have you ever had to read someone else's self-evaluation for an annual review? It's strange how our direct reports can't seem to properly identify their own weaknesses! Also strange is how our supervisors don't seem to agree with our own excellent evaluation of ourselves. (And give us the raise we so richly deserve).

The inability to have unbiased self-judgment was on full display each year during the *American Idol* auditions. Remember? Tens of thousands of potential superstars waited their turn to sing in front of celebrity judges. Every one of them felt they were good enough to win the competition. They genuinely felt they had the talent to impress the judges and sell records. Sadly, one by one, they had to be told: "You're not going to Hollywood. You're not a good singer."

Oh, the devastation. The heartbreak. But the viewing audience knew, and it was time someone told the truth. It is so hard to see the truth for ourselves. So if this is so hard—and perhaps impossible—to do, why do we do it? Because learning through accurate self-evaluation is so powerful. If you can honestly and fairly assess yourself, you are making the first steps to becoming unconsciously competent.

Gordon Training International:

Unconscious Incompetence: The individual does *not* know how to do something, does not realize their own incompetence, or sees no value in learning the skill.

Conscious Incompetence: The individual does *not* know how to do something, but now realizes their incompetence and sees the value in learning the skill.

Conscious Competence: The individual *does* know how to perform the skill. However, he must use great concentration and focused effort or process to complete the task.

Unconscious Competence: The individual *does* know how to perform the skill and is so practiced and proficient that the skill is "second nature."

The gradual development from conscious incompetence to conscious competence requires the student to talk through and evaluate their level of performance—and allows the trainer to observe and evaluate this process. The Johari window and other methods have shown that this concept of self-disclosure and reflection with others builds trust and powerfully develops awareness and skills.

THE COACH COACHES

When offering feedback, remember this phrase: Manage activity, not results. That is, focus on the behaviors and actions the trainee is exhibiting and NOT on the resulting feeling you have. It's easy to tell your trainee how you feel: "I didn't like your presentation." "Your speech wasn't effective." This sort of feedback comments on a result. You didn't like it and it wasn't effective. Your student is thinking, "fine, but what can I do to change it?"

The better feedback would be to direct the student on specific changes he could make in his presentation to make it more entertaining or effective. Manage activity, not results.

When I watch new managers or coaches give feedback I often see a common mistake: New managers will begin their feedback with an apology.

- "I'm not expert, but you could consider trying this..."
- "Listen, I'm sure you know more about this than me, but what if..."
- "You may want to try..."
- "It seemed to me that you..."
- "It kinda felt like you were..."
- "Your presentation was a little bit..."

These words (and others) only serve to communicate that you're not sure about what you're saying. When giving feedback, eliminate them. The result will be clear, focused, strong and effective feedback. Your trainees will thank you for it.

Drop these words:

- Sorta
- Kinda
- A little bit
- You may consider
- Might
- I felt
- Maybe

Just picture Bill Belichick, head coach of the New England Patriots on the sidelines of a football game that he is coaching. One of his players just fumbled the ball. As the player jogs off the field, Bill calls him over, "Hey, I noticed that you were sorta carrying the football a little bit too casually there. You may want to consider trying to hold it more firmly. I kinda think that would help us a little bit. Your thoughts?"

I don't think so. During this part in the ORBiT process, the coach coaches!

STATE THE POSITIVES

Have you ever seen the movie, *Meet the Fokkers*? It's the hilarious follow up to *Meet the Parents*, starring Ben Stiller and Robert De Niro. There's a great scene where De Niro's character (Jack) is talking with Stiller's father, Bernie (played by Dustin Hoffman). They're standing in Ben's old bedroom, in front of his "Wall of Fame": a collection of awards and accomplishments. Frankly, it's a testament to mediocrity. The exchange goes like this:

Jack: "I didn't know they made ninth place ribbons."

Bernie: "Oh yes Jack, they make them all the way up to tenth place."

Jack and Bernie have two different styles of child rearing. Bernie likes to support, encourage, and reward the effort regardless of the result.

Jack is only interested in achievement and result. In his world, reward is reserved only for those who achieve. In the world of feedback, it's important to begin with the positives:

- What worked
- What was right
- "That was good"
- "Keep doing that"

The purpose of this is not about helping your trainee to "feel better" or to manipulate.

I've often heard trainers attempt to "soften the blow" or cushion the negative feedback by starting with something good. This is referred to as a "praise sandwich" (or worse!). In a praise sandwich, the trainer would start and end with a compliment and squeeze the actual criticism in between. This technique is tired, transparent, and it simply doesn't work.

Here's an example of a praise sandwich:

"Jennifer, I love what you did with your hair today, it really looks great. Your speech was disorganized and ineffective. But I really liked the way you projected your voice."

This technique only serves to confuse the student and reduce your effectiveness. Instead, you should simply identify the actions that worked—what you want to see repeated—and call them out. Focus on the actions, not how you felt about them:

- Jennifer, your speech was exactly the right length. You finished in the time allowed.
- The opening to your speech was intriguing and had my attention right off the bat.
- Your voice tone and quality was appropriate for the room. I was able to hear you clearly from the back row.

Don't dress it up or invent false praise. If your trainee did something that you want to see repeated, just call it out. Nothing more is needed.

And know this: positive reinforcement isn't just a nice idea, it's truly important! Many of us are inappropriately focused on the negative. Why? Fear of failure. Avoiding danger. Concern over being embarrassed.

There is so much power in identifying and stating the positives. Once a negative statement has been made, most of us have a difficult time "unhearing" it.

- "You're so selfish"
- "You'll never amount to anything"
- "You're fat"
- "You're immature"

In fact, parents can validate that if you say to a child, "Don't spill your milk!" You can virtually assure that the child will, in fact, spill their milk.

How much more effective is it for us to tell our child, "Keep your milk on the table."

IDENTIFY THE OPPORTUNITIES TO IMPROVE

If you've been carefully following the ORBiT process, you are in step five: feedback. In order to gather evidence of your trainee's buy-in *and* skills, two things have happened:

- You watched as the trainee performed the skill in demonstration.
- You listened to your trainee evaluate their own performance.

Now it is your turn. Identify the specific behaviors that must change in order for the trainee to improve. For you to be effective at this, you have to know those skills. Even if you're an expert at performing these skills yourself, you will still have to be able to identify these skills from a distance, as a coach.

It's very difficult to see someone perform a task and offer advice that improves the performance. Have you ever played golf with someone who wanted to give you (unsolicited) advice as you were playing? Have you ever tried to incorporate their advice into your game, while playing? This usually spells disaster.

Shaquille O'Neal was one of the greatest players to ever play in the National Basketball Association. He won three consecutive NBA titles with the LA Lakers. Unusually big and tall, he was virtually unstoppable on the court. Unless he was shooting free throws. Shaq was one of the worst free throw shooters in history, shooting a paltry 53 percent. If you're a fan of the game, you also can remember that his poor statistics were validated by his incredibly poor shooting technique. Watching him shoot a free throw was painful for those of us on the sidelines.

It was easy to see he was uncomfortable and under stress. His free throw struggles were so widely documented that opposing teams were known to adopt a strategy called "Hack-a-Shaq"—designed to put Shaq on the foul line at crucial moments during the game, knowing he would miss.

Because of his obvious poor performance and low percentage results, numerous coaches and specialists helped him improve. Each one could see that something wasn't right. He held the ball badly. He stood awkwardly. He had no arch on the ball when he shot. Still, no coach was able to clearly identify and articulate an approach that was able to improve this aspect of his game.

In order for you to be effective in teaching the skills you want to teach, you have to be prepared. You must study behaviors. You must read, observe, validate, listen, and even try things for yourself to build a repertoire of coaching insights that help your students improve. The best sports coaches are doing this year round. In fact, learning their sport, the strategies, tactics, and techniques that win becomes an obsession to those that are the most committed.

Success at this level is not random. Improving another person's performance isn't accidental. It happens only when the coach is prepared, knowledgeable, informed, and focused. You must be perceptive at listening, observing, and gathering all the information you can in order to identify what will bring about improvement. Without this obsessive commitment to self-development and research, you are no different than the casual golfer giving out free advice to his playing partners.

DEMONSTRATE AGAIN

After watching your trainee demonstrate their version of the new skill you're teaching, you will likely see areas of potential improvement. During this feedback session, you're helping your trainee identify where they need to make corrections. You have to use all methods at your disposal to make your point. If there is opportunity, doing another demonstration (positive simulation) can be very effective to clarify where change is needed.

My son, Hank, makes a mean deviled egg. I guess it's a bit of a southern tradition. My sister Deidra taught him how. He had eaten so many of hers I guess she just wanted him to do it for himself. Watching her teach him was fun. If you don't cook deviled eggs you should know that it's quite an art form. There are lots of details and a wide variety (by region) of recipes. Being a bit of an expert on the topic, I can assure you the best of the best come from eastern North Carolina. One element of the process that must be completed perfectly is removing the outer shell from the egg. If you aren't diligent you will have holes or tears in the egg white that makes the presentation—as Deidra would say—unacceptable. When she was ready to teach, she had Hank stand next to her at the counter and showed him what causes the "unacceptable egg." Then, with a fresh, boiled egg, she showed him the (double secret) process for doing it right. Finally, while standing right next to him, she had him do it while she coached him through the process.

Of course, he had some questions. This is, after all, a delicate process. Time after time, he ruined a perfectly good egg. And, time after time, Deidra would patiently show him what he had done wrong. "You have to grab this inner membrane in order for the shell to come off smoothly." He watched. He tried. He failed. She's been doing it for decades—and this was his first time. It's hard to say just how many times she showed him (demonstrating again) what to do, but after an hour or so, he had it. He had learned—and replicated her technique and could repeat it time and time again. In the end, he had a beautiful plate of deviled eggs. Since then, he's our resident expert on deviled eggs. And he's batting 1,000. They're always tasty and done right (when there's any left over!)

Depending on what you are teaching, Demonstrating again may be the most effective form of feedback.

CLARIFY ANY MISUNDERSTANDINGS

"Clarify" is a good verb for our use. It literally means "to explain something more clearly so that it is even easier to understand."

Look back at the ORBiT process to see what has just happened: You, the coach, have just delivered feedback on your student's performance. Your student has conducted a "self-evaluation" of their performance. At this point in your process, you want to make sure that your student has actually learned what you are teaching.

I've raised four kids. Thankfully, all of them are now past their teen years. But, during those teen years I learned not to make one big communication mistake. The mistake is to not clarify what was agreed to. It could look like this:

Me: "Do you understand?"

Teen: "Yes"

or

Me: "Did you hear me?"

Teen: "Yes"

or

Me: "Do you know what I want you to do?"

Teen: "Yes"

I learned to add one more question to the exchange:

"So, what *did* I say?"

or

"Tell me what you *heard* me say"

or

"Good, so will you sum up our agreement before you leave?"

All of these are designed to follow up, to *clarify* any misunderstanding.

Over the years I've come to understand that when there is strong disagreement between people, there is usually a miscommunication at the root of the problem. In the context of business and leadership many people have a JWD misunderstanding. For our purposes, JWD either means "Job Well Done" or "Job Worth Doing."

Some misunderstandings exist because your student doesn't understand what a Job Well Done looks like. Picture this: You're the manager of a small retail store. Because you're a small business you ask one of your staff members to take their turn to clean the staff rest room. As you follow up one hour later, you find that the rest room is in disarray: The trash wasn't taken out, none of the chemicals have been used, and the toilet bowl wasn't brushed.

Here's your subsequent conversation with that employee:

"Bill, why didn't you clean the staff rest room as we had agreed?"

Bill replies: "But, boss, I *did* clean the rest room!"

You: "No, you didn't. It's a mess!"

Bill gets upset: "Well, I don't understand. I replaced the toilet paper roll and swept the floor. This is exactly the way I've always cleaned bathrooms before."

Ah, now we see the problem. Bill is more than willing to do the job. He just has a misunderstanding about what a Job Well Done is. I'm sure that once you clarify what *your* Job Well Done looks like, he'll be more than happy to do the job properly:

- Replace the roll
- Use cleaning solution to brush the bowl
- Take out the trash

- Sweep the floor
- Wipe out the sink
- Spray and wipe the mirror
- Replace and organize all supplies

When you clarify Bill's misunderstanding of what a Job Well Done is, you—and *he*—are on the same page regarding the job.

The other type of misunderstanding relates to whether or not a task is a "Job *Worth* Doing". In this case, your staff member doesn't do the job properly, because they don't see the value in the task. Let's revisit our previous scenario with this new type of misunderstanding. Once again, you have asked Bill to clean the bathroom. Once again, you follow up an hour later to find that the bathroom is not clean.

Here's your conversation with Bill:

"Bill, why didn't you clean the staff rest room as we agreed?"

Bill replies: "Something came up and I had to take care of that instead."

You: "Well, it still needs to be cleaned. Can you do it now?"

Bill digs in: "Honestly, do you really think I should be doing this? After all, I'm your best sales person. Shouldn't someone else be doing this so that I can go make sales?"

And, now we see the root of the issue. Bill didn't clean the rest room because Bill doesn't believe it is a Job Worth Doing. No amount of "training" will change this behavior, until you clarify this misunderstanding with him. He may not understand the value of a clean rest room for customer service, or he may not agree with you on the value of a team approach for store maintenance. This is a misunderstanding, and before you can move forward you must clarify the disagreement and make sure you and he see this in exactly the same way. If you can't, then this situation moves from a training issue to a disciplinary issue and you would handle that through your normal channels of discipline.

Before moving past this feedback session, you must check in with your trainee.

- Does he understand what you want?
- Does he understand what needs to be improved from his performance?
- Does he agree with your feedback?
- Is he clear about what you said in the feedback?
- Does he agree with your suggested approach?
- What is he going to do next?

Don't start into the "cycle" phase of the process until you have cleared the air, and clarified any misunderstandings your student may have at this point. This clarity allows you to make good progress and have a solid foundation for what is coming next.

CHAPTER SEVEN

"You must unlearn what you have learned"

— YODA

CYCLE

I'm sure you've heard the phrase, "Practice makes perfect." But this isn't entirely accurate. In a quote originally attributed to Vince Lombardi, but made famous by my good friend, Franco Zizzo, this concept is better stated as, "Only perfect practice makes perfect."

If your students are going to develop competence they must practice the skill in the correct way. So, in the "cycle" phase of the ORBiT process, we repeat the previous two steps:

- Demonstration (the trainee demonstrates the new behavior)
- Feedback (the trainer provides reinforcement and correction)

And we continue to repeat these two steps until our trainee consistently demonstrates the skill you're looking for. The cycle is the trainer's method of developing competence by "perfect practice." This takes place under the coach's watchful eye to make sure that the student is demonstrating the skills correctly. If this isn't done properly, the student runs the risk of adopting habits that will be very difficult to correct later.

A common example of this occurs as athletes begin a running routine. Too many people start a training regimen of running without supervision or coaching. Before long, they become frustrated by their inefficient performance and injuries caused by running with the wrong posture. Today there are many good-form running clinics that are dedicated to helping these runners unlearn their bad habits and improve their performance. It isn't easy because removing or correcting bad behaviors can feel counterintuitive and unnatural to what they're used to (that is, to the bad form that led to the injuries or poor performance). They would have been much better off to have "practiced perfectly" from the beginning.

But what is it that insures "perfect practice"? It's the skillful eye of the coach—you!—followed by the targeted feedback that corrects bad form or poor performance. This cycle phase of the ORBiT process is where proficiency is developed. Cycle is a specific word choice for this final phase. You can visualize the gears of a bicycle here: an ever-turning, continuous movement, first in one direction, then the other. The cycle phase refers to continuous development with an expectation of improvement: The student performs the demonstration, the trainer offers feedback. The student demonstrates again, and the coach offers feedback. The more this cycle is executed, the greater the development. Too many training exercises fail because they end before there is growth or a breakthrough. Students don't develop skills or become proficient simply because not enough time was invested in the cycle phase! Don't make that mistake. Complete the cycle until skills are developed.

Albert Alexander was the first patient who was given penicillin by Howard Florey in 1941. Albert had an infection that caused him to lose an eye and was causing him to have abscesses on his face. Florey administered the first dose of penicillin and Albert experienced an immediate positive response. After a few days, however, the supply of penicillin ran out. The infection was not completely destroyed; the antibiotic cycle was not completed. Albert Alexander relapsed and died a few weeks later.

While cycle is only the sixth, and final, step in the ORBiT process, it could easily be the phase that you will spend the most time on. The first five steps might take only a few minutes each. But once you get to cycle, you should remain here until progress is made and you see skills being developed.

DRILL

Repetition. The beauty of consistent repetition is that over time, muscle memory is increased and competence can be developed. Look at these words for competence which infer a history of repetition:

- Tenure
- Experience
- Seasoned
- Veteran
- Mastered
- Practiced
- Refined
- Polished

To develop competence we must practice.

I remember the first time I saw a typewriter keyboard. In the 1970s (when I was in high school) we still had manual typewriters, and learning to type was reserved for your sophomore or even junior year. (Of course, today what respectable elementary student can't successfully navigate a computer keyboard?)

As I looked at this keyboard, the location of the letters made no sense to me.

- Why is the "a" all the way over to the left under my left-hand little finger?
- Why is "j" so prominently featured under the first finger of my right hand?
- Why don't they just organize the vowels on the same row?
- Wait, you have to hit two keys to get a capital letter?

I can still remember how slow and awkward those first few typewritten pages were—and thank God for liquid paper! But, over time, guess what? It became more comfortable. More intuitive. As the months and years passed, I no longer had to think about where those letters were. My fingers just seemed to know where to go. By typing hundreds of thousands of letters (and immediately seeing whether or not my keystroke was correct on the page), I learned. I developed competence. I became... somewhat proficient. So, how long does it take to achieve this? Historically, it's been thought that it takes about 21 days of repetition to break or develop any habit. However, researchers at University College London have recently determined that it may take as many as 66 days to develop a new, successful skill.

As for your trainee, you have to create drills—simulations of the real thing—in order to see growth and development. Like a great coach of a team sport, you're on the sidelines, with a whistle, and the trainee is doing the work: learning, practicing, performing. You're observing, coaching, and offering feedback throughout the process. This is how competence is developed.

Let's now look more closely at the word "drill."

The military has "drill teams." These successful teams are a function of discipline and hard work. Hours and hours of practice result in precision, consistency, and sacrifice. In competition, it's the teams who are most precise and most consistent who win awards. One of the most inspiring components of a parade, state function, or military funeral is the performance of the honor guard. The exact escorting and presentation of the national flag is only accomplished through hours and hours of practice, sacrifice, and drills.

One of the most effective advancements in fire safety in the past 50 years is the implementation of school fire drills. Every state now has regulations requiring all schools to practice the systematic and rapid exit from the school building every month. During their school career, students will participate in a fire drill dozens of times. It is this very repetition that has dramatically improved fire safety for schools across the United States.

Karate skills are mastered using "kata" (literally means "form"). You may have seen these drills, where a karate student appears to be punching and kicking into the air as if they're fighting. There is no opponent. This is not a fight. But, with repeated practice of these exercises, the students master the forms and movements, which eventually become reflexes. This time-tested method of drills has worked effectively for thousands of years.

In fact, I will make the case that only those who commit to perfecting the drill will succeed when the actual skill is needed. Your task as the teacher is to devise the drill that will perfect the skill: Only perfect practice makes perfect.

One area of performance that has mastered the art of the drill is the marching band. So many elements must merge together perfectly for the performance to be appealing. For this to happen every band participates in band camp. Weeks prior to their first performance (usually a football game halftime show), the band will gather and begin to practice the fundamentals. Since they're performing on a football field, movement is usually organized in five-yard segments. Since most of the band's music is in 4/4 time, the band members must learn to cover five yards in eight steps. (I won't discuss the six to five option for you band veterans). While this may sound simple enough, I can assure you that it's quite challenging. So, in band camp, the band director must insure that drill after drill addresses this most basic band move. The entire band must be able to march five yards in eight steps--in perfect alignment, regardless of the various heights of the individual members or what size instrument they may be carrying. You can watch this on a video, read about it in a book, or listen to a lecture about it, but the only way to master it is to drill, drill, drill.

REVIEW/EVALUATE

Dan and the Neti Pot

Since moving to western North Carolina I have been plagued by a series of allergies. I have tried numerous medications and home remedies to alleviate the symptoms with limited effect. Nothing works long term. My Dad had good luck with a "neti pot" (a simple device that, I believe, may have gotten its start in Medieval torture chambers). He always recommended that I try it. The neti pot offers a straightforward concept: It irrigates, soothes, flushes, and hydrates the sinuses. Sounds good, right? What you may not know is the ungodly process the neti pot requires. First, you fill the pot with warm distilled water (plus saline). Second, you tip your head to one side. Now the fun begins. You insert the tip of the pot into one nostril and pour the water into your nose. Because your head is tipped to one side, the solution is supposed to proceed through your sinus and drain out of the other nostril!

"Desperate times call for desperate measures," I thought, so I acquired a neti pot and carefully read the instructions. Warm the distilled water. Check. Add saline. Check. Tip head. Check. Insert the tip of the pot into one nostril. Check. Enjoy the experience and find relief of symptoms . . . Not so fast.

The first time I did it, the water filled my sinuses and drained back into my Eustachian tubes, effective cutting off my breathing *and* my hearing. I thought, "This can't be right" and then quickly gave up the neti pot.

Fast forward a few more months of non-stop sinus trauma and I was desperate enough to try it again. Being careful not to pour too much water into my head, this time I was gentle. However, all I accomplished was to pour the solution into my sinuses and down the back of my throat (insert gagging sound here). The neti pot was returned to the cabinet.

This time I stayed away for a year. Only after a diagnosis of a sinus infection that had gone on for months did I become desperate again. The physician's assistant who worked with me insisted that the neti pot was effective and I needed to give it another try. This time I secured the help of my resident expert, Leslie. As a yoga instructor, HR professional, airline industry trainer, and long-time fan of the neti pot, I felt she was the right person to help me figure this out. I needed a coach.

As I stood over the sink with my Neti pot and began the process, she immediately stopped me. "Not only do you have to tip your head over, but you must also lean forward slightly."

"Am I not leaning forward?" I asked.

"Not far enough." She coached. "Lean over more." She continued, "Now keep your elbow horizontal with the floor. That's all you need."

Slowly, and perfectly, the cleansing solution poured into one nostril, navigated throughout my sinuses and exited exactly as it should from the other side. Success! Once I practiced this a few more times, I had mastered the process and have since become a fan and an advocate for the neti pot. For me to get to that point, I needed to rely on the experience, insight, observational skills, and coaching ability of Leslie Cunningham. Without her, I would not have had this breakthrough.

As you work through the cycle phase of this process, it's not uncommon for your trainee to get stuck. There is no progress. Skills are not developing. They can't figure it out. As much as you have set the context, and the trainee has indicated that s/he *wants* to learn and develop skills, it is simply not happening. Your role here is to be good at reviewing and evaluating what your trainee is doing. What do you see? Why isn't it working? What needs to change?

Here you would observe with insight and discernment. What do you see that you didn't seen before? You—and your trainee—are looking for a breakthrough.

Of course this is a lot of pressure on you, the coach. And that is why in any college or professional sport, it is the coach who is the last one to leave the office. The coach is studying. The coach is reviewing performance. The coach is looking at video of the team's previous games. The coach is evaluating statistics. What parable or metaphor will create a paradigm shift? What technique will make the difference? Mastering this skill of discernment will make the difference in your training role.

FEEDBACK

Here we are again. Feedback gets another section in the book! You could conclude that it must be important. You'd be right.

Most of what we do through the ORBiT process is done to give us an opportunity to offer feedback. Your feedback offers correction. Your feedback reinforces improvements. Your feedback illuminates mistakes. Your feedback identifies opportunities. Your feedback can create a breakthrough in performance.

At this point, you're in the sixth, and final, phase of the ORBiT process. The feedback "loop" takes on a new dynamic. If you've been successful to this point and your trainee is making progress, you should have engaged something in the student's motivation that has him actually seeking your feedback. This feedback process is not "one way." You should expect that your student is pulling information from you. They should be asking for your insight. They should be clarifying what you say, asking questions about it and actively engaging in the feedback process.

In fact, their reaction to the feedback validates that they are learning, engaged, and motivated to improve. If your student isn't engaging in this way (asking questions, seeking more information, requisition feedback), you may not have the level of collaboration it takes to make real progress. Over the years, I've found two primary types of mindsets that exist in the world: the "protective mindset" and the "achievement mindset." Most of the people I have led fall into one of these two categories. Let's have a closer look.

The protective mindset can best be described as people who are focused on simply protecting their job or their place in life. Most of their actions revolve around avoiding trouble, bypassing risk, and doing just enough to keep their job. These folks typically have a declining level of performance. When asked to do more, you'll often hear, "I'm not getting paid enough to do that!"

If you attempt to train or develop someone with a protective mindset, they're not going to be engaged in the process. You are asking for improvement and to do so goes against their very nature. Expect complacency, excuses, and passive-aggressive rebellion. The protective mindset might remain hidden throughout the ORBiT process up until this point. But if your student isn't engaging with you in the feedback process now, you may be working with someone who's not up to the challenge required to achieve improvement and growth.

The achievement mindset, conversely, is characterized as someone who is motived by growth. This person is driven to set and achieve goals. No matter what task is assigned, the person with an achievement mindset always seems to get it done. In fact, it is the very act of achieving that provides the inspiration. Therefore, this person *wants* to learn. This person is compelled to improve and surpass their previous performance.

So when you offer feedback to person with an achievement mindset, you can expect that this person will ask questions. This person will force you, the teacher, to be at your best. This student becomes your partner in their own improvement.

So check yourself at this point. If your trainee is *not* engaging with you, there could be two reasons why: Your student has a protective mindset and isn't motivated to improve, or your student has an achievement mindset—but you aren't providing insightful feedback.

As I write this, my son Hank is finishing up his teaching degree at Appalachian State University (go Mountaineers!). It's been fun to watch him learn the process of becoming a teacher. At first, he sat in class after class, while his teachers presented information to him. He then presented that information back to the teacher in the form of tests and reports, and the teachers offered feedback—whether he wanted it or not—in the form of grades. Over the years that process has evolved as he has become more and more responsible for his own development. This semester he's doing his student teaching. He has three supervisors through this process. Each of them are coaching him, reviewing him, and offering feedback. As Hank gets closer and closer to graduation he is simultaneously applying for teaching positions and being interviewed. Guess what? Hank is *asking* for more and more feedback. He sees what's at stake. He sees himself needing the help. He *wants* to improve, and so now he, the student, initiates the information flow. As a trainer, it is your focus to create—and expect—this same dynamic throughout your training as well. It is the very transition that has to happen for your student to master the skill and increase their productivity.

DEVELOP COMPETENCE

Herein lies the primary obstacle when influencing/training adults. Adults don't start with a clean slate. Before an adult can develop competence, they must unlearn what they think they already know. Unlearning is probably the most difficult part of the process for the student. A perfect example of this is in one of the first things we ever learn as a student: How to read. Students learn to read in the way that works best for them *at the time*. Over the years, however, most of us develop a series of bad habits that ultimately reduce our competence as a reader. Do any of these bad reading habits sound familiar?

- Sub-vocalization: "sounding out" each word in your head as you read them
- Reading word-by-word: concentrating on each separate word
- Poor eye movement: scanning across the sentence one word at a time
- Regression: re-reading sections to make sure you "got it"
- Poor concentration: usually due to self-imposed distractions

In order to advance your speed and retention in reading, you must overcome these habits. Of course, this is easier said than done—and explains why most people don't fully develop their reading skills. Developing reading competence requires that you unlearn bad habits: first, by being aware of them, and then by repeatedly working to develop new, effective skills that "override" the old habits.

One of the disciplines of developing competence is measuring your progress. This insures that your work is paying off.

In the world of speed-reading, there are two key metrics that matter:

1. Words per minute

2. Comprehension

If you intend to increase your speed and comprehension in reading, you must measure these two things. There are tests that can easily determine your performance in each category. In order to confirm your progress you must test at the beginning of your development process (to determine a baseline) and then you must regularly test throughout the development cycle in order to measure progress and confirm your approach.

You—the influencer, the coach, the trainer—must identify some way to measure the competence you're looking to develop. Everything that matters gets measured:

- Every book sold on Amazon is ranked by popularity (sales)
- Every student's GPA is measured to determine rank and identify the valedictorian
- Every baseball player is assigned a lifetime "batting average" to show how often they hit the ball
- Even a tree has rings to show how many years it's been around

If you are serious about influence, developing competency, and behavior change, find a way to measure the skill you seek to improve.

CHAPTER EIGHT

Decide

NOW WHAT?

So you've now learned the six steps of the ORBiT process: the Six Steps To Influence. Each of these steps is an effective leadership action in and of themselves. But, taken together, they are a powerful and effective approach to changing adult behavior and developing new skills. This process addresses the most difficult issue in adult behavior change: buy in. And this process systematically identifies your role in skills development.

Now what? Now it's time for you to decide to act. Note the root word here is "cide." You may recognize this root from a few other words, too: homi*cide*, sui*cide* geno*cide*, pesti*cide*. Yes, the common concept is death, to kill. "De*cide*," therefore, is a very strong word. Once you *decide* something, you have literally "killed off" all other options. There's no going back. You've made a choice and eliminated all other possibilities.

My recommendation to you is to stop making excuses. Stop allowing subpar performance from your team. Stop blaming. Stop being frustrated that you're not getting what you want from life. Stop feeling helpless. *Decide* to take action. Influence the adults in your world. Teach, train, develop, and coach your team until you have improved productivity and results. The opportunities to use your influence are everywhere.

Years before the advent of personal electronic devices I kept my daily calendar and contact list in a daily planner. I carried my planner in a nice leather notebook that was made by the great leather-goods brand, Coach. On a business trip to Portland, Oregon, I had inadvertently spilled some water on the cover and it became discolored in a few spots. This was a nice notebook, so I wanted to repair it. A business associate told me that I should go to the Coach store at Washington Square because the regional manager worked out of that location. He said I would be more likely to get something done there. I went into the Coach store at the Washington Square mall to see if there was a cleaning solution I could use to repair the damage.

As I walked in, there were two associates working in the store. I walked up to the counter. I was greeted with a warm smile and the associate said to me, "Good morning. My name is Ann. How may I help you?" I explained my situation: "My coach notebook has become discolored and I'm wondering if there is a solution to repair it."

Ann asked, "May I see it?" I showed it to her, and her response was immediate. "Oh my, this should not have happened. I'm so sorry." Ann looked back at me and said, "I'm going to need some help with this, can you excuse me?"

She walked over to the other associate and invited her into the conversation. "Janet, this gentleman has a notebook that has failed. Is there something we can do?"

Janet immediately took over and Ann went back to her project behind the counter. In the most supportive and professional way, Janet said, "This notebook is several years old, but still this shouldn't happen. I'm going to replace this notebook for you. Will you excuse me while I check our stock room? I need to see if we can find a suitable replacement."

I was stunned but happy with her offer. She stepped away briefly.

When Janet returned, she said, "Well, I have good news and bad news. I have found a new replacement for your notebook, but it is in our other store across town. I can't get it here until tomorrow." She continued, "I can ship this to your home, or if you can come by here tomorrow, I can have it here waiting on you. Which do you prefer?"

I was elated. She had solved my problem quickly and professionally. I chose the second option and let Janet know that I would come back the next day to make the exchange. She excused herself and indicated that she was going to set the transfer in motion.

While I waited, I stepped back over to Ann. "I guess it's nice to have the regional manager in your store to help with situations like this, right?" Ann looked up, "Excuse me?" I said, "Janet. Isn't she the Coach regional manager?" Ann smiled, "No, I'm the regional manager. This is Janet's third day."

Wow. Now I was truly impressed. Janet did, in fact, complete the transaction and the following day, I received my new, replacement notebook and left Portland as a lifelong fan of Coach—especially their retail stores.

Prior to my visit, Ann had done something special. She had invested time in Janet's development. She had taught her the vision for Coach service. She had shown her *how* to deliver that service. She had practiced this enough that Janet was able to execute that service with a customer. Sure, Ann could have easily handled the interaction. But, because of her investment in Janet, their business was better served, Ann's life was made richer, Janet's work performance was exceptional, and their customer is still bragging about this today—17 years later!

Now, you can choose to go on with life blaming your team for their underperformance. You can make excuses that others are lazy, clueless, uncommitted, or incompetent. *Or*, you can choose to do something. You can—you must—influence change. You can get the best out of your team. You can lead. You can influence adult behaviors, and as a manager/leader/owner/coach you must.

The ability to influence others has always been a powerful leadership skill. Just imagine always knowing that you can go into a performance environment where results are dependent on *you* and achieve! The powerful ability to influence insures that you will.

The ORBiT process is systematic. It's straightforward. It considers all the elements of successful adult learning. It is memorable and simple. All that is required is persistence. You will have to "call the meeting." You will have to implement the process. You will have to take responsibility. If you do, you will find a lifetime of opportunity. You will have a multitude of grateful team members who have been affected and influenced by your efforts. You will be in high demand as a leader who builds effective teams and gets results through those teams. You will be an Influencer.

POST SCRIPT

It's a rainy, cold day in Boston—early January 2017. I am on a break from training the fabulous staff at Landry's Bicycles. Todd Ouellette has finished reading this book and he's giving me his thoughts.

"I loved your book, Dan—very practical and right on point. However, I think you are missing one thing."

Of course I'm dying to hear his concern.

"Here's a key point—Once you have taught your team how to do something, you have to focus on maintenance. Measurement, follow up and consistency are the secrets to long term success."

I agree completely Todd. That will have to be my next book.

See you then.

ACKNOWLEDGEMENTS

There have been numerous people who have been most helpful to bring this book into reality. It's a shame to only give them a passing mention here, but suffice it to say, they offered invaluable insight, support, advice and feedback.

Franco Zizzo, Todd Ouellette, Tony Wolf, Fred Clements, Ryan Mc-Carty, Tony Tanner, and Rich Wills offered valuable insight into the approach, content and structure of this material.

Four leaders from Sun and Ski Sports were very important to me as they learned, mastered and implemented the ORBiT approach with significant success: Andrew Christ, Afua Giles, Kelly Knight, and Stan Paoli. You helped more than you know.

The owners, managers and leadership at Landry's Bicycles in Boston, MA taught me as much as I taught them about this approach. Thank you.

MY INFLUENCERS

It's impossible to acknowledge those who have significantly influenced me and brought me to this place in my life. But these are the people who have had the biggest impact:

—John Green. Uncle, mentor and best friend.
—Tom Laskowski. Constantly working to wake me from my sleep.
—Will Thompson. You told me what I had to do to write this book. You were right.
—Steven Covey. Your Seven Habits changed my life.
—Chip Heath and Dan Heath. Everything you write resonates with me.
—Malcolm Gladwell.
—John Heider. I've given away more copies of *The Tao of Leadership* than I can count. Still learning from this book.
—Leslie Cunningham. Cheerleader, editor, partner and inspirer. Seamlessly incorporating love, life and business. Tirelessly searching for ways to improve.

ABOUT THE AUTHOR

DAN MANN is a veteran of three distinct careers. He got his start in youth education as a schoolteacher, coach, choir director and youth pastor. He then worked his way through the retail world as salesman, regional management and buyer, culminating with a position as vice president of retail for Bachrach Clothing in Chicago, IL. Since 2003, Dan has impacted thousands of companies as the founder and president of The Mann Group, a consultancy based in Asheville, NC, where his clients include numerous Fortune 100 and Fortune 500 companies across the US, Canada, Europe and Asia. The common thread through these careers is simple: training. Dan has innovated, detailed and refined the process of influence to the benefit of businesses around the world.

CPSIA information can be obtained
at www.ICGtesting.com
Printed in the USA
BVOW08*0742250118
505360BV00001B/1/P